WYMONDHAM GRAMMAR SCHOOL

BRENDA M. GARRARD

for

WYMONDHAM HERITAGE SOCIETY

First published for the
WYMONDHAM HERITAGE SOCIETY
10, The Bridewell, Norwich Road, Wymondham, Norfolk. NR18 0NS
Registered Charity No. 299548
2010

ISBN: 978-1-901553-08-6

Previous works by the same author:

1990 Methodism in Wymondham

2003 Wymondham Parish Gilds in the Early Sixteenth Century

Printed and bound in Great Britain by
Print Services,
University of East Anglia,
Norwich. NR4 7TJ

Contents

Preface

This study of Wymondham Grammar School and its association with Becket's Chapel has been a natural sequel to my earlier research into Wymondham's Sixteenth Century Parish Gilds. It was the revenue from lands previously owned by the gilds which contributed most to the foundation and maintenance of the Wymondham Free/Grammar School, which for most of its life was housed in the gild chapel of St. Thomas Becket.

My interest in local history dates back to my schooldays at Thetford, and has continued throughout my teaching career. I was very fortunate to be able to join the first part-time M.A. course in Local and Regional History at the University of East Anglia in 1984. Most of my teaching has been in the independent sector, finally as a Headmistress and an Inspector of Mathematics. In the latter capacity, I visited many well-known independent schools, such as Rugby and Wellington, as well as smaller ones facing similar problems to those experienced by Wymondham Grammar School. As a governor of Thetford Grammar School for almost thirty years, I have been able to gain further insight into the organisation and maintenance of an independent school.

Brenda M. Garrard

February 2010

Acknowledgements

This book could not have been completed without considerable help from Wymondham Heritage Society, especially John Wilson, Mary Garner and Tony Wright, and from Adrian and Anne Hoare of Wymondham Heritage Museum, Janet Smith of the Wymondham Town Archive, David Pennel, Clerk of the Trustees of the Wymondham Grammar School Foundation, Vic Long of Priory House, Professor W. Y. Liang and Dr. J. Altham of Gonville and Caius College, Cambridge, John Webster and Anthea Iveson. I would like to thank them all, as well as the staffs of the Local Studies Library at The Forum, the Norfolk Record Office and the UEA Library.

All the older photographs have been kindly loaned by the Wymondham Heritage Museum, unless otherwise stated. The majority of the more recent ones have been provided by John Webster or the author.

I am greatly indebted to Julian Gillett for preparing the text and illustrations for printing. Finally, I would like to thank Roger for his constant encouragement and help, particularly with proof-reading.

To the memory of

PAUL CATTERMOLE

Introduction

A brief history of the Chapel of St. Thomas Becket up to the foundation of Wymondham Free/Grammar School in 1561

Foundation

William d'Albini, the second Earl of Arundel, and son of the founder of Wymondham Abbey, ordered the construction of the chapel one year after the canonisation of Saint Thomas Becket. It was completed in 1174, and dedicated to the Glory of God, the Blessed Virgin Mary and St. Thomas of Canterbury, for whom prayers and masses were offered. When d'Albini died two years later, two additional priests were appointed to sing masses for his soul and those of his ancestors. Prayers for the murdered Archbishop continued to be said, and in 1187 the chapel became the focal point of worship for the newly - established religious Gild of St. Thomas Becket, which continued to operate until 1538, when the gild became one of the first in Wymondham to close after threats by Henry VIII. According to documents in Wymondham Abbey, the chapel originally stood on open ground, the site of the town's first market place. It became the centre for pilgrimages from outside the town, and was apparently fenced off to keep careful control of its moneymaking potential.

The Building

The chapel itself was about 84 feet in length, 20 feet wide and 40 feet high. It contained a clunch (hard chalk) arch at the West end, a side chapel, a tower with two small bells, and a stairway to the Rood. Fortunately it was, like the Abbey Church, saved from destruction in the turmoil of the dissolution of the monastery, thanks to a royal grant and contributions from the people of Wymondham, who purchased its bells and the lead roof.

Repairs and early tenants

Between 1542 and 1547 repairs to the Chapel became necessary, and four original windows were replaced with those taken from the ruined Abbey. Two were placed in the chapel itself and two in the tower. Broken tiles were removed and replaced, as were flints, beams and roof timbers, many again coming from the old Abbey. More repairs to the windows were necessary in 1550, when the Chapel was rented out to the wife of Amos Kett. Subsequent tenants up to 1561 were William Francis and Randall Dowsing.

Additional buildings

Becket's Chapel has not always been the same as it appears today. Throughout its history, other buildings have been added and removed. One of the more important additions was the Town Shop, which was rented out, as early as 1547,

Becket's Chapel today. The fleur-de-lys over the door was the Grammar School badge, which is on all the buildings used by the school.

to John Davy. Other buildings attached at different times included the town lock-up and fire-engine shed.

The path to the foundation of Wymondham Free School

In 1504, there was a school in the town, probably connected with the Abbey. The schoolmaster at that time was William Irby, a monk, and brother of the vicar, Robert Irby. This school continued to operate up to and after 1538, in spite of the closure of the Abbey, but not in St. Thomas' Chapel, since, as we have seen, it was rented out. We know that in 1551 the headmaster of this school was Hugh White.

Gild lands to be used for education

In 1547, the first parliament of Edward V1's reign confirmed the closure of the town's twelve religious gilds, but promised that the proceeds from the sale of any remaining gild properties should be used for establishing schools for the education of boys.

The beginning of The Town Lands

We know that Edward V1 granted lands in Wymondham, which had belonged to the Gild of Corpus Christi but seized by the Crown, rent-free to Sir Thomas and Sir William Wodehouse of Waxham. In 1549, these two important political figures in the county returned them to the use of the town.

Although it was stated by Francis Blomefield in 1805 that the Wodehouses concerned had been from the Kimberley family, there were no members of the Kimberley Wodehouse family with these titles and names in 1549. A family tree, compiled by John Wodehouse, 1st Earl of Kimberley, printed in his family history, in 1887, confirms this, and Wodehouse himself states that Blomefield had made a mistake.

In the same year of 1549, several key inhabitants of the town met to discuss the future of the remaining gild lands. Some were then sold, the rest continuing to be rented out, as in the past. The latter, together with others given to the town for charitable purposes, became known as 'The Town Lands'.

More land changes

In 1559, a year after the succession of Elizabeth 1, John Flowerdew, the sole trustee of the lands and tenements once owned by the Gild of St. Thomas, surrendered them to the Queen, but they were returned to the use of the town in 1561 by Henry Blake, the chief steward of her manors and possessions in Norfolk, to key Wymondham inhabitants, namely

Thomas Hart	Robert Poynter	Robert Cushing
John Kensey	William Reve	William Kett
Valentyne Kett	John Cooper	John Foster
Richard Colman		

who were appointed to take and receive the profits and use them to pay a certain suitable master, 'fit to teach boys and youths', and to erect and maintain a school in the town.

1561,

therefore, was the year in which

WYMONDHAM FREE SCHOOL WAS FOUNDED

(later to be called the Wymondham Grammar School and the King Edward VI Grammar School).

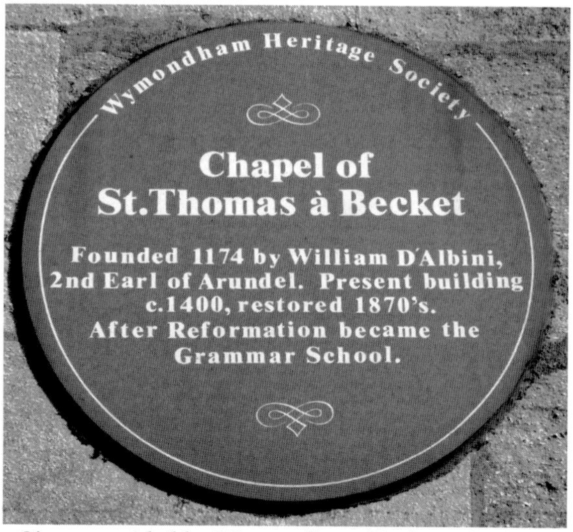

Sign, provided by Wymondham Heritage Society, outside Becket's Chapel

Chapter 1

Wymondham Free School: Early Years 1561 - 1617

The term 'free' grammar school has had several interpretations. Among these have been that of a school open to all who wished to attend, subject to no outside authority apart from the governors, and of a school not charging tuition fees. In Wymondham, although the school was open to all who wished to attend, reduction of fees was granted only occasionally to boys who came from the parish. The schoolmaster was paid from the income of the town's rented lands. Pupils' fees augmented this when necessary, and provided for day-to-day expenses, the cleaning and heating of the schoolroom, and making essential repairs.

Details of the early years of the newly established Free School in the town are very scarce, but we do know that it started operations in the schoolhouse near, but not in, Becket's Chapel, and incorporated any school already in existence.

Becket's Chapel

Although Becket's Chapel had been designated as the new schoolroom by the founders, it was not in a suitable condition. The early trustees did not act immediately to rectify the situation, and it was allowed to fall into further decay. Lead was even stripped from its roof. In 1570, complaints were made to the Privy Council by concerned Wymondham inhabitants, and, as a result, the building was eventually repaired and ready to be used for its intended purpose.

Early headmasters and pupils

As one would perhaps expect, headmasters came and went fairly frequently, as the success of the newly established educational venture was by no means guaranteed. The first name to appear in post 1561 documents is that of a Mr. James, who was headmaster about 1574.

Little is also known of early pupils, but George Jewell of Scoulton was the first boy on record to go up to Cambridge University from Wymondham Free School, and that was in 1565.

In 1600, these records also show that the first two students going to Cambridge from the town itself were Nicholas, the son of Nicholas Dickerson, a yeoman farmer, and Richard, the son of Edmund Bucke, a wealthy townsman. In desiring a university education the sons of the ordinary people were developing the aspirations of those of the gentry.

Oxford and Cambridge Universities

At the end of the sixteenth century these universities were very clerical in outlook, although subjects such as medicine and civil law could also be studied. The majority of the courses were designed for ecclesiastics, whether they wished to take holy orders or not. Boys would enter university from the age of fourteen to eighteen, eventually to qualify for the degree of Bachelor of Arts.

University Scholarships

Early students from Wymondham were encouraged to study at Cambridge University by a scholarship of £18, payable yearly for two grammar scholars, to Corpus Christi College, for which the Archbishop of Canterbury, Norwich-born Matthew Parker, had endowed the school. These scholars were to be nominated by the Mayor of Norwich, and chosen from scholars in Norwich, Wymondham or Aylsham. It is natural to suppose that the Mayor would consider Norwich pupils first, and indeed this appears to have happened, since the choice was challenged by Wymondham governors from time to time. Those fortunate enough to be selected were given 1 shilling per week for their 'commons', free reading, laundry and barber, and also allocated special rooms.

Charities merged

As early as 1583 the income from the gild lands to be used for the maintenance of the school had become merged with those left for the benefit of the town's other charities. In these comprehensive accounts, the schoolmaster's salary was by far the greatest expense, usually about one third of the total income.

The Seventeen

Who were the people who prepared and operated these charity accounts? By the mid-1580s a body of the most important parishioners of Wymondham had established themselves as a major administrative authority, representing both religious and secular interests. They had a wide range of responsibilities, including poor relief, highway repairs, binding apprentices, negotiation with outside authorities and maintaining law and order. This group of townsmen became known as The Seventeen, which was their total number, as revealed in the list published in 1604. They were also referred to as 'headboroughs'

However, this group of influential Wymondham inhabitants was not the same as that of the trustees, who were appointed to run the Free School, and this was often a cause of friction when important decisions about the school had to be made.

Market Street	Philip Cullyer Nicholas Dickerson John Moore
Damgate	Richard Dillon Stephen Agas
Town Green	Richard Rawlings
Chapelgate	Thomas Leverington gent.
Downham	John Symonds Edmund Barnard
Brawick and Stanfield	Henry Gay
Suton	Thomas Weld gent. Henry Blackborne gent.
Silfield	Stephen Wyseman gent. John Raven
Spooner Row and Wattlefield	Robert Day Edward Coleman sen. John Sheppard

Names of the Seventeen Headboroughs agreed at a meeting of the Townsmen January 3rd 1604

Headmasters from 1584

A father and son were both, at different times, headmasters of the school. Thomas Leverington was appointed from 1584 and stayed for five years, while his son, also Thomas, took over the school in 1603.

The Leveringtons were separated by Thomas Corbald and Simon Welles, both of whom were known in the town. Corbald came from Wortham, near Diss, and was the author of a book entitled *Kett's Camp*, while Simon Welles was the vicar of the parish from 1590 until 1607. He combined his parochial duties with those of headmaster, possibly from as early as 1591 until Michaelmas 1602, and was paid the set wage of £15 per annum. His move into education may have been necessary to supplement the rather low stipend of Wymondham vicars at this time, who themselves had to pay the wages of any curates they appointed. Welles withdrew from the school when he was also offered the Rectory of Crownthorpe in 1604.

Of the headmasters in charge of the school between 1606 and 1618, two stand out amongst the rest, a Mr. Castleton and Nicholas Easton. The former, who stayed only for a few months, may have been Henry Castleton, son of John Castleton, a Wymondham attorney, and an old boy of the school. Nicholas Easton stayed for five years, having come to the town with experience of teaching in similar schools in King's Lynn and Aylsham, and bringing some pupils from Aylsham with him. By this time, boys started going up to Cambridge University on a regular basis, and the headmaster's salary increased from £15 to £20 per annum.

Early Boarding / Rough Play in the Dormitory

At this time, boarding pupils were housed apart from the school, and the master's house may have been one of the buildings attached to Becket's Chapel, possibly a pre-1561 school building. An interesting payment recorded in the Town Book, for the replacement of mattresses for those which had been 'decayed' by the scholars, indicates that perhaps the nature of schoolboys has not changed over the years, and horseplay in the dormitory was not unknown in early seventeenth century Wymondham.

Other repairs

1603/4 seems to have been a busy time for repairs generally. The Town Book records quantities of sand, lime, tiles and bricks being transported to the schoolhouse, internal walls being mended there, and a wall being built outside it. Further expenses included the whitening of the schoolhouse and sheds, and for tile pins, nails and beer, the last item supposedly for the workmen, not the pupils!

Approval by influential people

By 1611 the school had apparently established itself in the town. The number of pupils now required the appointment of an usher as well as the master, and it was considered prestigious enough to educate the sons of Sir Charles le Groos of Wroxham, Sir Edmund Mundford of Mundford, three sons of the Wodehouse family of Kimberley and a relative of Sir Thomas Gresham. All these were destined to make their mark in the history of the county.

Perhaps the most famous was Edmund Mundford, who became a Member of the Long Parliament, which first met in 1640 and technically continued to be in session throughout the Civil War period. In 1646 he bequeathed 840 acres of arable land in Feltwell to trustees, for improving drainage there and establishing a free school, like the one he had attended in Wymondham. Unfortunately his plans came to nothing, as the drainage of this area, so close to the Fens, took all the income and sometimes even exceeded it.

The Great Fire of 1615

The schoolhouse of Wymondham Free School was destroyed in the fire which broke out on the morning of Sunday June 11th 1615. This was the timber building, adjoining Becket's chapel, which was used to accommodate the headmaster and the boarding pupils. Becket's Chapel, apparently, remained unscathed, but several other important buildings in the town were not so lucky, and suffered considerable damage.

According to the records of late 1615, the town already had a supply of wood assembled at Finderne, and although these oaks were originally intended for the poor of the town, it appears that many, if not all, were used for the rebuilding of the schoolhouse. This did not happen immediately, however, and the timbers were not moved, treated and assembled until the next year. Some of them may well have been used for improving the facilities of Becket's Chapel. Philip Cullyer, a wealthy Wymondham yeoman, loaned the town the sum of £30 so that repairs to the school could begin as soon as possible. Altogether about 1300 boards and 620 feet of boards were transported to the school, obviously very efficiently, since the carriers were rewarded with 5s 3d for 'dynners & for beere'.

Life in Grammar/Free schools in the early Seventeenth Century

Although our evidence for Wymondham is somewhat scarce, we can assume that pupils experienced the same procedures as those of similar schools at the time.

Boys usually entered these at the age of seven or eight. The only staff would be a master and the usher, an assistant teacher, although in a small school all the teaching was done by one man.

The working day was long, usually starting at seven o'clock and ending at five or six o'clock, with breaks for breakfast and dinner. Little time was allocated for play. Schoolmasters were not encouraged to arrange this. Between five and eight weeks in the year were allowed for holidays.

Strict discipline

Discipline was strict. Flogging and being pulled by the ears were accepted methods of punishment, and masters were sometimes accused of brutality. School regulations required parents to place their children unreservedly in the charge of a schoolmaster and they were not expected to interfere in the disciplinary process. In fact, pupils would be dismissed if their parents objected to the master's correction. In the schoolroom, prompting and helping others was a more serious crime than failing to do well. Older boys were sometimes appointed monitors.

The curriculum at this time

Boys could usually write before they entered the grammar/free school. Sometimes a visiting master would help those lacking such skills. Arithmetic was rarely taught before 1660, and was often considered unnecessary after that, as it was not required for university entrance. Indeed, it was considered more suitable for those entering trade. Latin grammar was still a key subject in the seventeenth century, although the practice of speaking in Latin was beginning to die out. The study of Greek continued to be important, and sometimes Hebrew was included. Schools were encouraged to set up libraries, although the number of books in them remained very small, as they soon became worn out or were stolen. Wymondham Free School purchased a Greek Lexicon in 1617.

The day began and ended with prayers, and on Monday mornings pupils often had to give an account of the sermon they had heard at church on the previous day. Masters were allowed to devise their own teaching methods, but were forced to lecture, with little input from the pupils, when the class was large.

More headmasters

The period following the departure of Nicholas Easton in September 1614 and the events in 1618 is somewhat unclear. No schoolmaster seems to have been paid for six months, after which time a Mr. Brown received the customary wage, although not at the usual times. In 1617 a Mr. Firmary appeared on the scene, but he was paid for 'teaching the scholars', rather than being referred to as 'the schoolmaster'. It is possible he was a pupil at that time and used as a temporary usher. Later evidence would support this view.

Chapter 2

The years 1618 - 1640

Henry Peacham, a very important headmaster

Although in the post for not much more than one year, Henry Peacham must lay claim to being the most famous headmaster of all, and responsible for putting Wymondham on the national map. He is still referred to today by serious Shakespearean scholars.

Who wrote *Titus Andronicus*?

There has always been some dispute as to whether William Shakespeare was the original author of the play *Titus Andronicus*, or whether it had been written by the Earl of Oxford. There is no need for us to look into the details of this argument here, but it is relevant to consider some of the people who have contributed to it.

Who signed the document?

One of the key documents in the dispute is that which has become known as 'The Peacham Document'. It takes its name from a signature written on the left side, 'Henricus Peacham' (see picture) which is followed by a date transcribed as 1574 by one side of the argument, and as 1594 by the other. If the true date was 1574, then the document was signed by the father of the Wymondham headmaster. If the date were 1594, it was presumably signed by the headmaster himself. The majority verdict seems to be that it was the father's signature, but this detracts nothing from the son's importance.

Henry Peacham senior, associate of Queen Elizabeth 1

Henry senior was a clergyman, responsible for the souls of the parish of St. Mary in North Mimms, adjacent to Hatfield House, a favourite visiting place of Elizabeth 1. This Henry was obviously a man of letters, who moved in the highest circles of society, and was a regular visitor to Hatfield House at the invitation of the Queen. Here he met Michael Hicks, secretary to William Cecil, who became the possessor of the famous document, which contains a scene from *Titus Andronicus* with a very important ink drawing at the top, to which we will refer later.

Henry Peacham, junior

Henry junior, born in North Mimms about 1575, went to Cambridge in 1593, and became an even more important figure in English history than his illustrious father. He showed a very early interest in drawing, which turned out to be the subject of his first book, *The Art of Drawing with the Pen*, for the instruction of 'the young learner', published in 1606. He had to overcome considerable opposition to his studying art, and writes with feeling of the beatings he had taken from his schoolmasters for sketching his classmates in Latin Grammar lessons. His tutors told him that he had been placed in their care to be made a scholar, not an artist. It is quite clear that Peacham never enjoyed his role as a teacher, but was forced to recourse to it throughout his life, as he failed to find a wealthy patron. He wrote that teaching was unrewarding and 'one of the most laborious callings in the world'.

Connection with Shakespeare - the first illustration

Experts believe that Henry junior was responsible for the pen and ink drawings at the top of the Peacham document, which is commonly accepted to be the very first illustration of a Shakespeare play. But his talents did not stop here, and he was also very interested and skilled in mathematics, music, poetry and literature. He composed emblems, or short poems, and presented a few to James 1 in 1603 as he travelled down from Scotland on his accession to the English throne. Between 1603 and 1610 he completed three books of emblems, two dedicated to Prince Henry and one to the king.

Arrives in Wymondham

After a period in London, Henry travelled in Europe, published other works and sought employment again on his return in 1618. His previous teaching experience made him extremely suitable for the role of headmaster of the Wymondham Free School, and no doubt the chief inhabitants of the town were flattered that such a famous person should apply for the post. One can only assume that at any interview he kept his views on the rewards of the teaching profession to himself.

He must have taken to his work, his pupils and the town very rapidly, as he published a collection of short poems, *Thalias Banquet,* whilst in Wymondham. Some of these contain interesting references to local places and pupils. Number 30 reads,

Windham I love thee, and I love thy soil
Yet ever loathed that never ceasing toil
Of thy faire schoole whilst that it was free
Myself the master lost my libertie

Other poems are dedicated to pupils, Edward Chamberlain of Barnham Broom, John Cook of Deopham, and Hammomd Claxton. Unfortunately his stay in Wymondham did not change Henry's opinions on teaching, and he left after one year, to return to London. In 1622, his most famous work, *The Complete Gentleman,* was published. This was dedicated to William Howard, third son of

Enter Tamora pleadinge for her sonnes going to execution

Tam: Stay Romane bretheren gratious Conquerors
Victorious Titus rue the teares I shed
A mothers teares in passion of her sonne
And if thy sonnes were ever deare to thee
Oh thinke my sonnes to bee as deare to mee
Suffiseth not that wee are brought to Rome
To beautify thy triumphes and returne
Captive to thee and to thy Romane yoake
But must my sonnes be slaughtered in the streetes
for valiant doinges in there Cuntryes cause
Oh if to fight for kinge and Common weale
Were piety in thine it is in these
Andronicus staine not thy tombe wth blood
Wilt thou drawe neere the nature of the Gods
Drawe neere them then in being mercifull
Sweete mercy is nobilityes true badge
Thrice noble Titus spare my first borne sonne
Titus: Patient your self madame for dy hee must
Aaron do you likewise prepare your self
And now at last repent your wicked life
Aron: Ah now I curse the day and yet I thinke
few comes within the compass of my curse
wherein I did not some notorious ill
As kill a man or els devise his death
Ravish a mayd or plott the way to do it
Accuse some innocent and forsweare myself
Set deadly enmity betweene too freendes
Make poore mens cattell breake theire neckes
Set fire on barnes and haystackes in the night
And bid the owners quench them wth theire teares
Oft have I digd up dead men from theire graves
And set them upright at theire deere frendes doore
Even almost when theire sorrowes was forgott
And on theire brestes as on the barke of trees
Have with my knife carved in Romane letters
Lett not your sorrowe dy though I am dead
Tut I have done a thousand dreadfull thinges
As willingly as one would kill a fly
And nothing greeves mee hartily indeede
But that I cannot do ten thousand more

Henricus Peacham
Anno m°q°q°to

So far from Shakspere Titus Andronicus Sc. 2

The famous Peacham Document. Note the signature Henricus Peacham and the unclear date on the left hand side. (Reproduced by permission of the Marquess of Bath, Longleat House, Warminster, Wiltshire.)

the Earl of Arundel, who, with his two older brothers, had been tutored by Peacham in Norwich.

Peacham and Blickling Hall

On a recent visit to Blickling, I discovered that a set of plates, copied from the drawings of Henry Peacham's *Minerva Brittanna* (1612) were the basis for the series of emblems which adorn the plaster work of the Long Gallery ceiling, repaired in the 1620s.

Headmasters 1618 to 1640

After the high profile of Peacham, information about his immediate successors is somewhat limited. A Mr. Cudworth followed him in 1619 for two years. This was probably the Rev. Daniel Cudworth, of Emmanuel College Cambridge, who was not ordained until 1620. John Gibbon, possibly of Bury St. Edmunds, stayed a little longer, from 1621, but we cannot be certain when he left as our source, the first part of the Town Book, ceases in 1622.

More documentation is available for the period of leadership of the Rev. William Locke (1627-1640) at a turbulent time in England, as politicians and clergy began to take sides in the disagreements between King Charles I and his Members of Parliament. Locke, ordained a priest in Norwich in 1628, became Rector of Tibenham in 1638, and appears to have managed the dual occupation of priest and Wymondham master fairly successfully, sending an average of at least one pupil to Cambridge every year. We do not know what prompted him to leave the town, but he was replaced in October 1640 by Francis Wildman.

1635 Inscription

In 1635, during Locke's period of office, a Latin inscription was placed over the main door of the school.

Ano. Dni 1635
Musarum Aedes Wymondhamenses
Ne Pulsate fores
Sint tecta Silentia Musis

The exact purpose of this is not clear, but, roughly translated, it reads:-

In the year of our Lord 1635
The Wymondham abode of the Muses
Beat not the door
Let the retreat of the Muses be quiet

In later years, a replica of this inscription was mounted on a board and hung inside the main school building.

Gan/Gunn/Gang Monday

In the early seventeenth century, preachers regularly visited the town for Rogation week. On the Monday before Ascension Day, there was a procession through the town, in which the pupils of the Free School took part. This day was referred to as Gan, Gunn, or Gang Monday, and was no doubt eagerly anticipated by the boys, as they were rewarded with beer and cakes afterwards, which were provided by the town authorities.

The Market Cross would have been a central feature of the procession. (reproduced by permission of John Wilson)

Chapter 3

Civil War, Commonwealth and Restoration

Controversy in the church

We are now reaching the period immediately prior to the Civil War in England, and, although not in the main battle areas, the people of Norfolk, and indeed Wymondham, held their own views about the antagonism between King Charles l and his Parliament.

Successive Bishops of Norwich had the unenviable job of trying to control the two extreme views of Puritanism and Catholicism, and maintain the established Church of England in their diocese. They demanded that the list of preachers be printed and published, both in the parish church and on the notice board in the Chamber at the Griffin Inn. Pressure was also put upon the ecclesiastical authorities to allow the appointment of a 'lecturer', a battle eventually won with the appointment of John Money. Clergy who held too extreme views were turned out of their livings.

Throughout the reigns of Queen Elizabeth and King James 1, the Puritan movement had been gathering strength with the ordinary people of Norfolk. The Catholic plots against Elizabeth, the Spanish Armada and the Gunpowder Plot, reminded them of the burnings of Protestants in England by Queen Mary and the continuing tortures of the Catholic Spanish Inquisition on the Continent.

The support of Catholicism in the area came mainly from the gentry, who did not want their political authority challenged by the local Puritans.

Reactions in Wymondham

How did these problems affect Wymondham Free School? It could not avoid being affected, since clergymen had to be licensed by the Bishop, and statutes insisted that the Master of Wymondham Free School had to be a clergyman. Some priests who had been ejected from their livings by the Bishop or by national authorities, because of their extreme religious views, now became available and were very willing to become schoolmasters in order to earn a living. Two of the leading Norfolk gentry, Sir John Hobart of Blickling, the lord of the manor of a large part of Wymondham, who educated his two younger sons at the school, and Sir Thomas Wodehouse of Kimberley, its chief trustee, both had Puritan sympathies, and they held considerable influence when it came to appointing a schoolmaster.

1640 and Civil War

They obviously used their influence when Francis Wildman was appointed in 1640. His brother John, a clergyman in Diss, was known to be a strong supporter of Puritanism, and it was assumed by the authorities at the time that Francis was of a similar inclination. His views do not appear to have prevented the school from growing in numbers, thereby creating the need for an usher, Mr. Door, to assist the headmaster, who was anxious to complete his MA that year.

Even more headmasters

In 1644, Wildman was replaced by William Matthews, the son of a Mendlesham husbandman, ordained in Norwich in 1640. In 1645, he paid £5 for the rent of a house in Vicar Street, which he used for himself and his boarders. Unfortunately, we do not know exactly where this was. Matthews died 'in harness' in 1647 according to the burial register, and his widow was granted 14s 8d of Parliamentary money.

Another Puritan supporter, John Firmary, followed next, in 1647. He had been recently ejected from his living at Beeston, which suggests that his religious views did not exactly coincide with those of the local church officials. However, he seems to have been acceptable in Wymondham, and was grateful to find suitable employment. It is possible that he was the same John Firmary who had been a pupil, turned usher, at the school in 1617 and thus returned to an area where the family held land. He stayed for a period of three years, in the last of which he was assisted by an usher, Mr. English, who came to deal with an increased number of pupils.

The Commonwealth Period

What determined Firmary's departure is not known. In fact, records are generally rather incomplete for this period of the school's history, because of the continued religious turmoil. The Civil War ended in 1649, when King Charles 1 was beheaded, and Oliver Cromwell, a well-known Puritan leader, took over the reins of government. It seems likely that Thomas Bradford, a fellow Puritan, born in Norwich, was appointed headmaster in 1651.

Keeping an eye on the Wodehouse family

An unusual part of Bradford's brief, on appointment, seems to have been to 'keep an eye on' a member of the Wodehouse family who was beginning to develop too Royalist a view for the local authorities, and the new master was presumably encouraged in this by some of the Wodehouse family themselves. His additional appointment as Rector of Kimberley gave him every opportunity to monitor the movements and opinions of the unfortunate person concerned.

The removal of politically incorrect schoolmasters

Bradford's stay in Wymondham coincided with the attempt by the Puritan, Commonwealth government to control religious education in schools by the setting up of the Commission for the 'Ejection of Scandalous Schoolmasters'. As the wording implies, those schoolmasters not conforming to the government rules and beliefs of the day were forcibly removed from their posts. They were considered to have too much influence on the young pupils. Thomas Bradford left the school in 1653, but his departure was not connected with this legislation. He may have remained as Vicar of Kimberley for a little longer.

After that he followed the pattern of other clergy at this politically troubled time, by moving between the church and the schoolroom. In 1656 he was appointed Rector of Winterton, where he experienced some problems at the restoration of the monarchy, and later became master at Great Yarmouth School.

A drawing of Kimberley Hall. Sir Thomas Wodehouse (1585 – 1658) allowed the old Hall to fall into disrepair. This picture is after 1754.

His career ended back in his birthplace where he was curate of several churches and chaplain of the City Gaol. Rather disappointingly, Thomas Bradford does not appear to have had complete confidence in the Wymondham Free School during his time there, and preferred to send his son, another Thomas, to be educated at the Norwich Grammar School.

Richard Ransome, appointed in 1653, found the buildings had been somewhat neglected, and immediately set about repairs to the masonry. His move from the church into education may, once again, have been for theological reasons. His previous church appointments included those in Gresham, Cromer, Ingworth and Alby. His son, another Richard, received part of his education in the town, where he was joined by Robert Gallard, the son of the Rector of Wreningham, who spent eight years at the school, went to Cambridge in 1656 and returned six years later to become headmaster.

The Colman Scholarships

In 1659 Edward Colman, a gentleman of Norwich, left £20 per annum to Corpus Christi College towards the maintenance of four pupils - two from Norwich and two from Wymondham. His interest in Wymondham came from the fact that he owned lands and tenements in the town. His family name was obviously very important to him, and he made a special caveat to his bequest. If there was a student named Colman/Coleman among the applications, then the whole sum of £20 was to go immediately to him, and any existing grants would become void. If, on the other hand, there were no applicants, the executors were given authority to spend the money in whatever way they felt suitable!

Headmasters of the Restoration period

The year 1660 saw the restoration of the monarchy, after the failure of the Puritan government. There were changes in Wymondham as well as in the country as a whole. The first headmaster of the reign of Charles ll, Anthony Jermy, arrived in the town and left almost immediately to become the Rector of Gunton, near Cromer. Robert Gallard, an old boy of the school, is named in the Diocesan records as taking over the school in August 1662 and staying for a similar short time, before moving to become the Rector of Cranwich, dying there in 1667, a young man of twenty-seven.

From 1663 the Wymondham Town Book records the appointment meetings of headmasters, which enables us to be certain of their dates and lengths of stay in the town. These committees were overseen and usually chaired by the local gentry, and always included at least one member of the Wodehouse family. The first of these was Henry Tyrell, a graduate of Trinity Hall, Cambridge, who began his period of office on March 1st of that year. He seems to have set about his duties energetically, and made considerable repairs to the schoolhouse. John Morphew followed five years later. He was already the curate in the town, and his stay of four years would probably have been much longer had he not unfortunately contracted smallpox in 1672, from which he died.

A very successful headmaster

In June of the same year Morphew was replaced by Richard Clarke, curate of Mileham, near Scarning, who went on to become one of the most successful headmasters Wymondham Free School ever had. He was also appointed curate in the town, a post which he probably held until his death in 1707. No doubt he found the headmaster's salary of £20 per annum a useful supplement to his meagre wage as a curate, although he held other clerical positions in the area – Rector of Intwood from 1680 to 1707 and Vicar of Ketteringham from 1697 until his death in 1707.

A new headmaster's house

One additional benefit Richard Clarke enjoyed over his predecessors was the provision of a house for himself, his family and the boarding pupils. This was the result of a bequest contained in the will of Robert Dey, proved in 1672, and the house, now known as Churchgate House, was a substantial one, which could accommodate several boarders. It was very conveniently close to the schoolroom, with just the Green Dragon Inn between them. If the headmaster did not wish to live in the house, then, under the terms of the will, it could be let out, and the rents used for binding out poor apprentices in the town.

Special Pupils

If Richard Clarke's success can be measured by the background of his pupils and the number of them going to Cambridge University, then the school was certainly enjoying a period of prosperity. Two of the earlier pupils were John and Thomas Hobart, the youngest sons of Sir John Hobart of Blickling Hall. This is not perhaps as surprising as it would at first appear, as the Hobart family had inherited extensive lands and possessions within the town, including the manor of Grishaugh, which comprised approximately 1800 acres and represented about one third of all Wymondham lands. Most of it lay to the east of the town. The only remaining reference to its name is preserved in 'Gristlewood', a moated and wooded mound, clearly visible today from the new Hart's Farm estate.

Although the presence of these two boys enhanced the reputation of the school, it is unfortunate that Sir John's eldest son and heir was sent to Thetford Grammar School, which was much older and boasted of a pre-Norman Conquest foundation. John and Thomas, born only one year apart, did well at Wymondham Free School. Both went to Sidney Sussex College, Cambridge, in 1682, and then to Lincoln's Inn to study law. John later became a Brigadier-General in the King's Army and is buried at Blickling, while Thomas died unmarried, and does not seem to have distinguished himself sufficiently to be worth noting in the family histories.

Churchgate House in Church Street, bequeathed to the school under the will of Robert Dey.

Other important pupils

Several other pupils at this time came from families well-known in the community. Martin Jubbes, James Seaborne, John Talbot and William King were all pupils from the town whose fathers were described as 'gentlemen', while several of the local clergy, including one from Hingham, chose to trust Richard Clarke with the education of their sons. Perhaps parents were encouraged by the fact that Richard Clarke had sufficient confidence to educate his own two sons, Hezekiah and Roland, at the school. Thornagh Gurdon, whose father, Brampton, was another gentleman, residing at Letton Hall, also became a pupil, and went on to become the Receiver General of Norfolk. He was called into the school later, in his professional capacity, when a dispute arose over the appointment of Clarke's successor. Another interesting pupil was Peter Gleane, who managed to survive the impoverishment of his father's estate and his resulting stay in the Fleet Prison. He later succeeded to his father's baronetcy and became Proctor in the Court at Canterbury.

Over forty-five pupils went to Cambridge at regular intervals during Clarke's thirty-five years of rule. The College of Gonville and Caius became the main aim of most young men from East Anglia, unless there were family connections and loyalties to other colleges. This is particularly helpful as the alumni records

Blickling Hall, the home of the Hobart family.

for Gonville and Caius have been thoroughly and carefully researched by J. Venn, enabling the progress of these students and their subsequent careers to be followed closely.

Loss of Vital Documents

On September 17th 1679, it was admitted by the town's authorities that all documents relating to the school's foundation, including that of the procedures for the appointment of new trustees, had been lost. Lawyer Mr. Lewis Linton, was called in by the 'chief inhabitants' to assist them in re-instating the old trustees and appointing new ones. Under Mr. Linton's guidance, it was agreed that Thomas Weld, Thomas Talbot and 29 others, who had to be either inhabitants of the town, or landowners in the parish, should comprise the new voting authority. This was agreed, and all went smoothly until January 1707, when Richard Clarke died while still in office, at the age of sixty-seven.

Assets of Richard Clarke

This death was naturally a shock to all. The inventory of Richard Clarke's goods, made after his death, reveals that he died a comparatively wealthy man. In addition to all the furnishings necessary for his family and the boarders in the eighteen rooms of the new schoolhouse, his possessions included silverware and about two hundred and fifty books. The total value of this inventory, including debts, was £229 15s 6d, which certainly compares favourably with his annual salary of £20.

Gonville and Caius College, Cambridge. Many students from Wymondham went up to study here during Richard Clarke's time as headmaster.

Chapter 4

Disputes in the town

The appointment of the headmaster – 2 vital questions

Clarke's death was a considerable blow to the school. In order to continue the education of the many boys attending, George Taylor became headmaster. Taylor had been vicar since 1701, and this was probably considered a temporary measure at the time. Although there was not the usual formal election and appointment meeting, Taylor duly subscribed under the Bishop's regulations for teachers on February 21st 1707. All was not well, however, and disputes began to arise as to who should elect the schoolmaster.

Two questions needed answering. Was Mr. Linton correct in appointing the 31 trustees, and should they or the chief inhabitants of Wymondham elect the schoolmaster? During the next year another learned lawyer was consulted, a Mr. Bransby, who affirmed the right of Mr. Linton to appoint the trustees. He said that, since twenty-nine years had elapsed without any dispute, Mr. Linton was justified in his actions, which he did not consider could be challenged in a Court of Law, unless there was some evidence of fraud or abuse.

On the other question, of the right of election of the Schoolmaster, whether it should be in the hands of Mr. Linton's trustees or in those of the chief inhabitants of Wymondham, Mr. Bransby, on July 19th 1708, stated that it would be:

> *monstrous that the trustees should have the trouble and trust of managing and improving, but not disposing.*

In other words, he supported the legal rights of the existing trustees, and said at the same time that it was allowable for them to pass on their voting rights to others.

More lawyers called in

These statements did nothing to settle the dispute, and it continued apace. In August of the same year some leading inhabitants of Wymondham called in the services of two well-known attorneys, Walter Bacon of Earlham, Norwich, and Thornaugh Gurdon of Cathedral Close, who, as we have seen, happened to be an old boy of the school. They were asked to advise the town of possible procedures for electing a new schoolmaster, which could be used on all future occasions.

After listening to all parties and inspecting written evidence, the lawyers decreed that the remaining trustees should hand over their powers of administration of the Town Lands and rights to elect the new schoolmaster to a group of men who either lived in Wymondham or who owned land there. These were to number thirty-one in total, thus adhering to the number previously decreed. It was perhaps a fairer representation of opinion within the town, since approximately half of the existing trustees lived outside the parish and many could not claim land ownership.

Final Statement

These directions were confirmed on 28th October 1708 by regulations which stated that, when 16 or more trustees should be dead or removed out of Norfolk or Norwich, a public notice should be given appointing a general meeting to fill up the trustees to 31 again, choosing people of Wymondham or those owning land there.

The outcome of these legal negotiations and disputes surrounding the appointment of a schoolmaster was an end to the existence and influence of the 'select vestry' which had dominated secular parish administration for over a hundred years.

Vicar versus curate

In spite of the legal activity, almost a year later nothing of significance appeared to have actually changed. George Taylor continued in office, and it was not until 24th May 1709 that matters moved ahead, when Mark Pert, the curate, was elected headmaster. His tenure of the post lasted only two weeks, until a public meeting of 83 of the 'chief inhabitants' elected Taylor to continue. Many of these were working-men of the town, and twenty-seven of them made their mark rather than sign the resulting document.

George Taylor seems to have finally been accepted and the formal appointment meeting was held on June 6th. Mark Pert moved to become Vicar of Great Finborough. Whether or not this was a case where the vicar pulled rank over his curate we do not know. No doubt the additional salary was attractive, but George Taylor continued at the school without problems until 1712, when he resigned, without clear reasons, a controversial figure until the end.

What happened to the school during these tempestuous times?

There is no evidence to suggest that the education of boys did not continue, but recruitment and scholarship must have suffered with all the controversy. No boys appeared to go to Cambridge during this period. The whole episode was such a contrast to the times of Richard Clarke's successful rule.

Taylor was succeeded by Isaac Sayer, one of the headmasters to be honoured with a memorial in Wymondham Abbey, which was apparently provided by his devoted wife, when he died at the early age of thirty-six. He was the son of a Norwich weaver, but appears to have owned small amounts of property in

The Town House is believed to have been this house in Vicar Street.

the area. We do not know what caused his early death, but he certainly worked hard during his lifetime, combining his duties as a schoolmaster with clerical positions in Crownthorpe and Bradenham, as well as a curacy in Wymondham.

A Charity School in the town

It does not appear that the Free School was the only academic institution operating in the town at this time. Records show that a property, called the Town House, in Vicar Street, was rented by a John Benett in 1718. While he was there it was referred to as the Charity School. A notebook relating to Hendry's Charity in the Wymondham Town Archive shows that a charity school was indeed operating for much of the eighteenth century, but the next tenant of the Town House was Edward Durrant, a linen weaver, indicating that the school must, by then, have moved elsewhere.

The assets owned by the Wymondham Town Lands Charity

In 1719 a list was compiled of all the assets owned by the Wymondham Town Charity. It included 53 acres of arable land, 12 acres of meadow and 26 acres of pasture. Buildings in its possession included Becket's Chapel, Churchgate House, the Town Cellar, the cellar under the school, the town shop and eight tenements, three of which were on The Lizard. (See table on page 81)

Joseph Brett, a controversial figure

Another Norwich-born and Gonville and Caius scholar succeeded Isaac Sayer. Joseph Brett took over the responsibilities in March 1721 in what appears to have been a quick and efficient exercise by the trustees to limit the time the school was leaderless. There is no evidence in the Wymondham records to leave any doubt that Brett was a hard-working and efficient headmaster.

In his fifteen years in Wymondham, he sent at least fifteen pupils to Cambridge, one of the first of them being William Wodehouse, the elder son of Sir John of Kimberley, who unfortunately died prematurely, before his father, and left his younger brother Armine to inherit the baronetcy. Another well-connected pupil of his for one year was Thomas Gooch, the son of the Right-Reverend Bishop of Bristol and Master of Gonville and Caius College, Cambridge. At this stage, the weakness in Joseph Brett's character, revealed in documents relating to his next post in Scarning, could not have been evident.

Scandal at Scarning

According to a pupil at Scarning named Thurlow, who was later to become Lord Chancellor in the Government of William Pitt, on one occasion Joseph Brett threw a slate at a pupil and knocked him out. Realising what he had done, Brett rushed out to get water to bring the unfortunate pupil round. The remaining class was divided as to whether it should try to help the unfortunate pupil or not. Some pupils did not want to help him, hoping that he would die and then Brett would be hanged. The headmaster was certainly not a popular figure, and this does not appear to have been a singular incident, since he is recorded as having been dismissed for cruelty in 1750. Nevertheless, he found favour with the church while at Wymondham, and held the united rectories of Kimberley and Carleton Rode, both in the gift of the Wodehouse family.

The dilapidation of the headmaster's house

During Brett's period of office, the state of the headmaster's house deteriorated to such an extent that he said it was uninhabitable and moved out. By an earlier Indenture, the Head was expected to keep the house in good repair at his own expense, unless he were a single man with no family, in which case the property was to be let and the profits used to pay for a poor child to complete a trade apprenticeship every year. The responsibility for ensuring that the premises were maintained satisfactorily, in accordance with this indenture, was given to the trustees in Robert Dey's will. Unfortunately, these trustees had omitted to fulfil their obligation in this respect, and when Edmund Blackborne, the last remaining of the original trustees, died, the responsibility for putting the matter right fell to his surviving heir, Anne Blackborne. She petitioned the group of new trustees for the property to be repaired out of the rents and profits accumulated, in accordance with the will.

There is no evidence to suggest that the necessary repairs were carried out. Indeed we can assume they were not, since headmasters appointed in 1778 and 1790 are recorded as having refused to live in Churchgate House, because of its dilapidation. This could not have encouraged the recruitment of boarders. Were they expected to live in such conditions, or were they also housed elsewhere?

Maintaining the number of Trustees

A recurring problem of the Eighteenth Century was that of ensuring that, when the number of trustees had fallen to sixteen, it had to be increased to thirty- one, as decreed by the rule of the 28th October 1708.

A meeting was called in March 1736 when their numbers had reduced to a mere seven, namely:

Sir Armine Wodehouse	Samuel Proctor	Bartholomew Dey
Thomas Turner	John Stephenson	Harry Bidewell
Simon Bishop		

Its purpose was to elect sufficient numbers to fill the places of all those deceased.

At this meeting, John Wodehouse, Rev. Philip Wodehouse, Thomas Wodehouse, Rev. Richard Drake, Rev. Randall Burroughes, Rev. Peter Petit, John Stoughton, Peter Stoughton, John Talbot, Antony Ransome, Robert Wigg, James Carver, Clere Sewell, James Burroughs, Randall Burroughs, John Drake, Thomas Burroughs, Ellis Burroughs, Robert Stoughton, John Clarke Stoughton, Gamaliel Ransome, Thomas Talbot, John S. Cann and George Mann were all selected to become the new trustees.

The number of members of the Wodehouse family in this list is quite usual and illustrates the influence the family had in the school's affairs.

Collection of Rents

The collection of the rents of the town lands and their distribution, according to the established rules, was a very important responsibility. The management of the Free School was only a part of this, although the largest individual sum paid out annually was that for the schoolmaster's salary.

The accounts were kept by a treasurer or receiver, elected by the trustees and responsible to them. Records show that, during the eighteenth century, those holding office were:

1726	Thomas Randall, a wealthy brewer
1736	Jeremiah Burroughes
1767	The Rev Randall Burroughes
1772	The Rev Richard Drake John Stephenson Cann

Repairs to the school

Although the headmaster's house had become neglected at this time, the trustees were more efficient over the state of the school itself, and several repairs were carried out. Glazing continued to be a regular feature of these, but it is not clear whether or not the necessary work was the direct result of over-active pupils.

Map of the Town Lands

In 1773 the trustees paid a certain Mr. King to undertake a complete survey and draw up a map of all the town lands. This task was duly completed, but the results went missing, at some later date. This led to Edward Pomeroy, a trustee at the time, undertaking the same task himself. In 1892, he presented the trustees

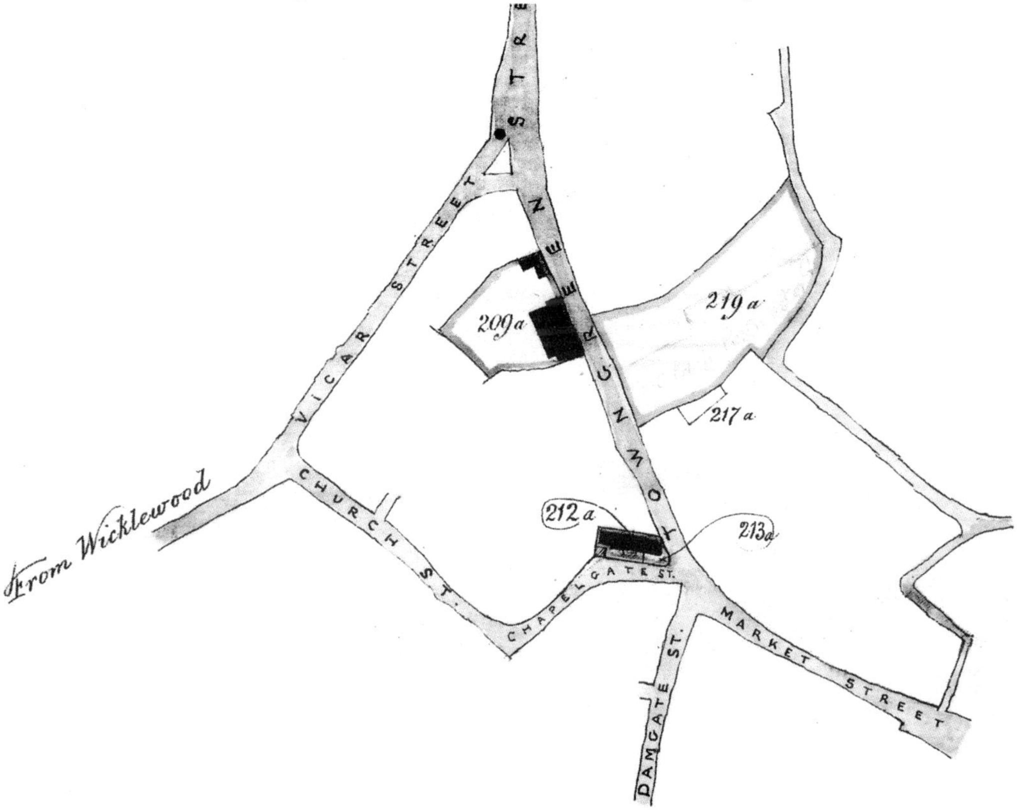

One of the maps drawn up by Pomeroy. Number 212a - Becket's Chapel, 213a - the Town Shop, 209a - Priory House, 219a - the acre of land opposite which was used for sport and recreation.

with a book showing all the Grammar School lands and those of the Fuel Allotment Charities, which he had compiled.

More headmasters

A very smooth transition followed the departure of Brett for Scarning in 1735, he being replaced by William Evans almost immediately. The new headmaster had also held several church positions, including the rectories of Ilkeshall St. Margaret, Crownthorpe and Great Hockham. During his period of office, in 1746, Caius House was built on land abutting the northern boundary of the school

Comparatively few students went up to Cambridge or Oxford during his twenty years of rule, but competition became greater as the universities, now no longer solely for the training of clerics, began to attract a wider range of students.

William Evans died 'in harness' in 1755, and there followed another period of uncertainty and disruption. After a gap of two years, when the school may have continued under an usher, a disastrous appointment was made. Frederick Matthew lasted from February 1757 until Michaelmas of the same year, and died from mental problems at North Walsham five years later.

One year after Matthew's appointment, Thomas Langham restored stability to the school. Already known to the population of Wymondham as its curate, Langham may have helped to run the school in the previous gaps, before his official appointment. Few details are available of Langham's work, but his combination of the two posts merited a memorial in the Abbey. The inscription, roughly translated, reads:

> *The monument and tomb of the Reverend Thomas Langham, schoolmaster of this town, well educated in academic pursuits at Pembroke College, Cambridge. He became well known for his intellect and literary works, he was an apt and elegant speaker and he was an effective persuader. He lived well and died bravely on 17th May 1768 at the age of 44.*

Another two-year break

It was a pity that Langham's obvious good work in the school was followed by yet another break of two years before his replacement could be found.

Joseph Hepworth, appointed in April 1770, was obviously a man with clear aims. He came to the town from North Walsham, and, on the day of his appointment, an advertisement appeared in the *Norfolk Chronicle* making his intentions clear:

> *Wymondham Free Grammar School. The Rev. Mr. Hepworth, Assistant to the Academy at North Walsham, being appointed Master of the Free*

Grammar School of Wymondham proposes opening the said school at Midsummer next; where young gentlemen may be conveniently boarded and instructed in the languages, writing, arithmetic and every branch of mathematics.

The advertisement suggests that the school was actually closed for some time, rather than just being leaderless. Perhaps some of the previous pupils returned, but it must have been a difficult choice for parents who would have liked their sons to be educated in the town, but were loath to move them back if they were settled elsewhere, remembering the disruptions the school had suffered in the past. It is also interesting to note in the advertisement the school is now being referred to as a Free Grammar School.

Hepworth certainly got things moving, and several repairs were made to the schoolhouse (Churchgate House) between 1772 and 1775 by carpenters, joiners, glaziers, masons and bricklayers. The total cost of the work was a high proportion of the £70 annual revenue from the rents of the Town Lands, and emphasised the lack of further endowments to fund the school. Unfortunately, Hepworth's success with the Wymondham Free School did not profit it in the end, as he was recalled to North Walsham in 1778. Even more bad news followed when it became known that he was taking some pupils from Wymondham with him.

Another new headmaster

Fortunately, his successor was appointed without delay, indeed in the same month that Hepworth left, and for once the transition ran smoothly. He was probably well known to at least one trustee, who wrote to his fellows that the Rev Thomas Taylor was:

a proper person to be a master of the said school.

The Curriculum

The customary advertisement appeared in the *Norwich Chronicle,* informing readers that the boarding fee was 18 guineas per annum and 1 guinea entrance. The subjects to be taught were Latin, Greek, writing and arithmetic, a return to the emphasis being placed on the importance of the classical languages. Like his predecessor, Taylor refused to live in Churchgate House because of its condition.

Other appointments

During his period of office, he, like many previous headmasters, also fulfilled church appointments, being curate at Ashwellthorpe 1780-84, rector of Bracon Ash 1787-1804, and perpetual curate of Cringleford 1787-1804. He left the school in 1788 after exactly ten years, and died at Eaton in 1804, while still comparatively young. We can learn little of his work at Wymondham, but the ongoing repairs to Becket's Chapel indicate that the school was operating with some success.

One wonders how the school continued to operate in Wymondham with yet another gap of two years before a successor was found. It says much for the character of the incoming heads that they were able to build up numbers to make the school financially viable. It is difficult to discover how similar schools fared in this respect, but at Norwich Grammar School the line of headmasters continued without interruption.

The end of the Eighteenth Century

Roger Buston arrived to take over in March 1790, on the increased salary of £30 per annum. It may well have been the low salary of £20 per annum, little more than the £15 originally set in 1561, which had failed to attract a headmaster in the intervening two years. Another problem had to be faced - that of the condition of the headmaster's house. Like his predecessors, Buston refused to live in it until the house was put in 'tenantable order'. Buston originally came from County Durham, but moved to Norfolk to become curate of Necton and Holme Hale in 1786, from where he would have seen the advertisement for the post. Rather surprisingly, he is also recorded as having been Rector of Great Barford in Bedfordshire from 1789 until 1817. Considering the distance involved, and the state of the roads at this time, he must have employed a very efficient curate.

The *Norfolk Chronicle* contained its now familiar advertisement on June 12th 1790, stating that Mr. Buston would be opening his school on July 12th, where:

> *young gentlemen will be genteelly boarded and assiduously instructed in the Latin and Greek languages, History and English Writing, Arithmetic, Algebra, Geography and the use of Globes.*

It would have been impossible for one man to have taught all these subjects, and other staff would have had to be employed, although restricted by financial considerations. There was certainly a visiting dancing master and probably an assistant, Joseph Rivett, who appears on the Norwich Subscription lists at this time.

Class differences

The advertisement also distinguishes between boarders at £20 per annum and 'parlour boarders' at £30 per annum, confirming the existence of a class structure within the school. Parlour boarders lived with the family and were treated as part of it, which must have caused some problems with the relationship between pupils. The cost of sending a pupil to the school would already have restricted the intake to those of relatively prosperous means. Buston appears to have been a successful headmaster, if one looks at the type of pupils he attracted to the school. An article which appeared in the *Gentlemen's Magazine* on his death confirms this suggestion. Two pupils, John Stephenson Cann and Edward Palmer Clarke, sons of important Wymondham men, were educated at the school at this time, and later played important roles in its continued development. The 'Magazine' describes Buston, at his death, as a man of profound erudition.

More famous scholars

The school also attracted the attention of wealthy and influential families outside the town, and the famous Diary of Parson Woodforde, of Weston Longville, reveals that, in June 1792, William and Charles, the two sons of Parson Woodforde's friend, the priest at Reepham, were pupils at the school.

Where is the door today?

A view of the south side of Becket's Chapel. The doorways have been blocked up at some time in the past.

Chapter 5

The Nineteenth Century to 1884

A long, leaderless period

Roger Buston died, while still headmaster, in 1817, and in October of the following year John Hardy Raven was appointed to fill the post. Having just been appointed a priest, Raven may have thought it useful employment while he searched for a living in the church. For whatever reason, he did not stay long, and by the end of 1818 the headmastership was again vacant. There followed the longest period of closure of the school, which would certainly not have helped its standing in the community or the county.

There does not appear to have been any sense of urgency in advertising for a replacement. More than two years later, in February 1821, an application was received from the Rev. Edmund Roberts of Woodrising, who had heard of the vacancy. He quotes the Rev. Papillon (Vicar of Wymondham) as a referee. By December of the same year, there was still no appointment, and complaints were made in the town. A letter from Mr. William Cann, voicing these concerns, was sent to the trustees, but they were either unwilling or unable to proceed further.

It was not until 1825 that the post was advertised and applications were received. Among these was one from Thomas Kidd, who had been Second

On the left, an early picture of Priory House. The acre for sport is opposite.

Master at Merchant Taylors School for seven years, followed by six years in charge of the Grammar School at King's Lynn. He had exceptional references, including those from the Masters of four Cambridge colleges, who described him as 'one of the best classical scholars in the kingdom'. The Wymondham trustees were therefore well aware of the advantages of appointing such a prominent figure, and made every effort to attract him to the town.

That they were successful was apparent when the following advertisement appeared in the *Mercury* for June 10th 1825:

> *The Reverend Thomas Kidd M. A., late master of the Grammar School of King's Lynn will commence school business on 2nd August 1825. The terms for accommodation of boarders and co. may be known by applying to the Reverend T. Kidd at King's Lynn. Young gentlemen as parlour boarders prepared for universities.*

Thomas Kidd was not a young man when he came to Wymondham, and was probably in his fifties. A completely different description of him, from the one quoted in his references for the post, was given by Mr. Jessop, a contemporary local historian, who described him as:

> *If not too good for this world, he was too simple, childlike and absorbed in his studies to make an effective schoolmaster. His career was a sad one.*

He certainly proved to be a well-respected scholar, and his later appointment as headmaster of Norwich School in 1829, together with the many references written by former pupils and parents, indicate that Jessop's judgement of Kidd was a little harsh.

Important changes

The conditions that the headmaster had to be a clergyman of the Church of England, and be qualified to teach Latin and Greek, were still in operation, and an additional provision was now added, that the headmaster could not be the Vicar or a curate of the parish. It seems that the authorities had learned from experience not to mix the two positions. To compensate for this, and to obviate the need for additional income, the salary was raised from £20 to £60.

Attention was also paid to buildings. Churchgate House had continually been in a state of disrepair, and many heads had refused to live there. Rather than spend sums which they could ill afford on putting the house in order, the trustees were able to negotiate a deal with Cornelius Tipple, a prominent business man in the town, in which they exchanged it for what is today known as Priory House in Middleton Street, together with an acre of land on the opposite side of the road, which was intended for the pupils' playground The name 'Priory House' is somewhat misleading as it has no connection with the former monastery, but was tenanted by a family with the name of Prior in the 1920s.

Sign outside Priory House. The foundation date is open to question.

Repairs and renewals

Priory House then became the new schoolhouse, but unfortunately it did not come without its problems. Under the terms of the appointment, the Kidds were responsible for repairs during their occupancy, and this was to sour future relations between the headmaster and the trustees.

Bills to Mr. Kidd for 30,000 bricks indicate that much building work on the new school house was undertaken in 1826, in addition to repairs. A new laundry was constructed, and the total bills to be paid amounted to almost £300. Settlement of these dragged on, and in desperation, when they were almost two years overdue, Mrs. Kidd wrote to the clerk of the trustees asking them to be

One of the rooms of the original Georgian house. Note the lightwood panelling.

The rear view of Priory House. The building on the left was added when the school moved here.

settled, at the same time commenting on the dilapidations in the schoolroom, tables and forms, when they took over.

Mrs. Kidd, whose nursing skills were appreciated by the pupils and parents, was partially successful in her appeal, and Baron Wodehouse, chairman of the trustees, contacted the school's solicitors to release the Kidds from almost half the sum. Unfortunately this was not until 1830, by which time the Kidds had left Wymondham.

The time and concern spent on these financial matters must have had some impact on the efficiency and smooth running of the school. Mr. Kidd subsequently was three years at Norwich, and died in 1852. In his later years he was awarded a government pension of £100 p.a. for services as a scholar and instructor.

Thomas Kidd was succeeded by George Cubitt in 1830, but only for a short time. Another graduate of the University of Cambridge, Cubitt may have already been in the school as an usher. The existence of a letter from Lord Wodehouse to the remaining governors states that he had seen Cubitt and felt that it was unnecessary to advertise further for a headmaster. This suggests that Cubitt was already known to the governors, who had agreed that he should take over in the absence of a more suitable candidate.

A former pupil at Norwich School, Cubitt had been ordained in the city in 1829. In retrospect his appointment was not a wise one, as he did not stay beyond the end of 1830, the year in which he had been appointed. He then returned to Cambridge, was awarded his M.A. in 1832, and followed it with a trip to India and a stay in Madras in 1834. Once again, the school was left without a headmaster.

At the end of 1830 notices appeared in *The Times* and *Morning Herald* once more inviting applications for the post of headmaster. There was considerable interest shown from all over the country, but not all prospective candidates continued when the details of the post were forwarded to them. Perhaps the salary was insufficient for their desires or needs. The final number of applicants was five.

A headmaster from Oxford

One candidate, Richard Kirby, was able to supply many references but no testimonials. One reference describes him as having 'kept a highly respectable classical school in Bath', and the governors were sufficiently impressed to appoint him. Richard Kirby's stay in Wymondham broke the continuous chain of headmasters from Cambridge. A graduate of Exeter College, Oxford, and originally from the West Country, he arrived, ready to start operations, in January 1831, having advertised his pending arrival in the *Norfolk Chronicle* in the November of the preceding year. His statement of proposed fees makes interesting reading.

The charges for boarding and education were fifty guineas per annum, which covered everything apart from books, tradesmen's bills and medical attendance. Each boarder was expected to arrive with a silver tablespoon, knife and fork, and six towels. No deductions were allowed for occasional absence.

One noticeable event, which occurred in 1835, during Kirby's time, was the school's move to the newly refurbished Priory House in Middleton Street, already being used for boarding accommodation. This left Becket's Chapel to stand little used for more than fifty years.

Mr. Kirby leaves in haste

There are no ways in which Mr. Kirby's effectiveness as headmaster can be measured, since one of the previous methods, of using the number of students progressing to Cambridge, was no longer valid. The automatic path from free grammar schools to the universities was no longer being followed in Wymondham, as in the country generally.

It appears that Kirby left Wymondham rather suddenly for London in 1838, as a result of a period of ill health. Elizabeth Kirby was left to conclude the practical arrangements, such as the transport of furniture, and negotiations with the governors for the payment of his salary. Some governors felt that Kirby's illness was brought about by over-work, as he had combined his duties in the school with a chaplaincy and a curacy in an attempt to increase his income. No longer allowed to hold these posts within the town, he had looked elsewhere, and became the curate at Crownthorpe, which offered him £50 per annum, not much less than his remuneration from the school.

Another vacancy

Once more the school was leaderless, and it was not until October 24th 1839 that an advertisement for a new headmaster appeared in *The Times*, as well as in regional papers in Norfolk and Bury St. Edmunds. The delay for this is unexplained, but it meant, once again, that pupils would have to attend other schools and were unlikely to return to Wymondham when a new head was found. The advertisement included the usual stipulation that applicants had to be a clergyman and from Oxford or Cambridge, and promised them a salary of £60 p.a. with a good house and garden.

Although there were a few applications, no appointment was made, and further advertisements appeared in April and July 1841. The latter of these resulted in eight applications from as far as the north of England as well as a local one from the Rev Edmund Roberts of Woodrising, who was supported by a past Wymondham vicar, the Rev. William Papillon. One applicant, the Rev. Charles English of Budleigh, Somerset, later withdrew his application due to 'the long vacancy injuring the school'.

No additional appointments available

In an attempt to avoid the over-expectations of candidates to supplement their income by additional appointments, the governors investigated the availability of such responsibilities and the incomes they provided for potential headmasters. They passed this information on to all applicants. In a very candid letter to the Rev. C. Bird in Bolton, Lancashire, the clerk stated that the:

> *late master, Mr. Kirby was by no means successful here and he held during the whole of his residence a chaplaincy and a curacy.*

He then points out that both of these positions were filled and likely to remain so, so that any future headmaster would be entirely dependent on the school for his income. About this time the governors were rather surprised to receive a letter from the Rev Kirby, asking for:

> *re-instatement to his former position after his affliction, now that he is restored to perfect health.*

They did not respond positively.

More class distinction

Newly-appointed Robert Slipper arrived in the town in August 1842, with definite ideas as to the type of school he wished to lead and the background of the boys he wished to educate. His forthright views soon created some concerns amongst the governors. A firm believer in the merits of advertising, he announced his arrival in the *Norfolk Chronicle* in 1842,

> *'The Reverend R. B. Slipper, Master of Wymondham Free School, will receive pupils on January 31st on the following terms. Pupils to be educated in the school 60 guineas per annum. Gentlemen reading for Ordination or for the Universities. Private bedroom or study 70 guineas per annum.*

Further indication of his concern for the social standing of his pupils is revealed in a letter to the clerk of the governors, John Mitchell, who had informed him of potential new pupils likely to join the school on his arrival. Slipper warned the clerk not to send any, such as a certain ten-year-old boy called Richard, who are:

> *not respectable enough for a Free Public School, and might injure the school's reputation.*

Joins a rival school

In fact it was Slipper himself who probably did more harm to the school's reputation than his pupils, as in late 1842, what must have become a familiar sight to the inhabitants of Wymondham was yet another appearance in the local paper of an invitation for prospective heads to apply for the vacant position of headmaster. To exacerbate the situation, Slipper was moving to the school's nearest rival institution, Hingham Grammar School, and probably took some pupils with him. There had always been some competition between the two, and some pupils of Hingham School travelled from Wymondham daily.

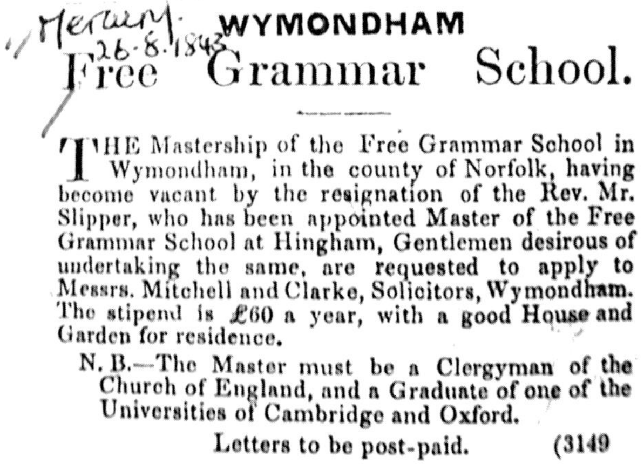
Mercury. 26.8.1843

WYMONDHAM

Free Grammar School.

THE Mastership of the Free Grammar School in Wymondham, in the county of Norfolk, having become vacant by the resignation of the Rev. Mr. Slipper, who has been appointed Master of the Free Grammar School at Hingham, Gentlemen desirous of undertaking the same, are requested to apply to Messrs. Mitchell and Clarke, Solicitors, Wymondham. The stipend is £60 a year, with a good House and Garden for residence.

N. B.—The Master must be a Clergyman of the Church of England, and a Graduate of one of the Universities of Cambridge and Oxford.

Letters to be post-paid. (3149

Advertisement in the Mercury dated 26th August 1843

Among the applications for the vacant post was one from the Rev. Joseph Grisdale, who had been the Sub Master at Norwich Grammar School for 3 ½ years. His testimonial from the headmaster there described him as having:

> *high classical attainment, great facility of communicating instruction, industry, energy, perseverance, amiable deportment and strict integrity.*

Another testimonial, this time from Grisdale's Vicar, the Rev. C. W. G. Parker, said he had doubled the number of services, attracted crowded congregations, and that they would be very sorry to lose him. Again, Wymondham hoped that he would prove to be an asset to the school.

Losses in the Wodehouse family

In 1846, the Wodehouse family and Wymondham Grammar School suffered a joint loss. On 29th May, Sir John Wodehouse (2nd Baron) , died. He was succeeded by his twenty-year old grandson Sir John Wodehouse (3rd Baron and 1st Earl of Kimberley), his son Henry having pre-deceased him by twelve years.

The new Baron, John Wodehouse, must have become only too familiar with unfortunate deaths in the family. Between November 1833 and February 1835, his twin sister, a younger sister, his father and his paternal great grandfather, all died. As well as the 10,000 acres in Norfolk he inherited, there were also several hundred acres of land in Cornwall. Although he became very involved in the work of the House of Lords from the 1850s, rising to the position of Lord Privy Seal, John Wodehouse was also very active in the locality of his birth. He often served as Chairman of the Quarter Sessions, and as a trustee to various schools and parish boards. In Wymondham, he continued the work of his predecessors, by becoming Chairman of the Grammar School's trustees. For his

John Wodehouse, first Earl of Kimberley (1826 - 1902)

contribution to state affairs, he was rewarded by the title of Earl of Kimberley.

Reduction of numbers

In 1868, there were 31 boys on the school roll. These included 11 foundation scholars, who were paying only £2 per annum, instead of the usual £6. The trustees commented that this was rather below the average number of pupils there had been in the school previously. In 1864, there had been 50.

Further dissension regarding appointment of trustees

A letter to the Charity Commissioners, dated 16th September 1868, reveals that there was some controversy in the town regarding the appointment of new trustees. A meeting was organised by four townsmen, who had failed to be nominated themselves, to object to those who had. The majority of leading parishioners refused to attend when they saw,

> *the class of persons of whom the meeting was chiefly composed, some of them being paupers in receipt of relief*.

In a discussion of the superior social standing of landowners compared with those engaged in trade, typical of the period, the existing trustees felt that no shopkeeper should be a trustee. This meant that William Standley, Jasper Harvey Tipple and John Robert Smith could not be considered.

Objections were also made to the appointment of Mr. Finlay, the surgeon, who, it was maintained, could not always attend meetings, as he needed to travel extensively in the parish. Others not acceptable were tenant farmers and those who were nominated by shoemakers. In another communication, William Taylor, a dealer in corn and coals, was also considered to be ineligible because the greater part of the yearly income of the fuel/allotment charity was expended in the purchase of coals.

Further repairs necessary

In 1869, in spite of the reduction in pupil numbers, the trustees were forced to consider spending money on property. Cottages adjoining the 'Old School' (Becket's Chapel) were purchased by William Clarke, and the trustees became very interested in acquiring this property in view of its proximity to the Chapel. Neglected since the move to Priory House, the Chapel was now in desperate need of repair. A letter was sent to the Charity Commissioners, asking permission to spend £827 out of the School's Charity Funds for this purpose. This sum was to cover repairs inside and outside the building, as well as furniture, fittings, lights and heating, and to make it usable for school purposes once more. Apparently, application for such repairs had been submitted as early as 1855, when the plans had been drawn up by Mr. Thomas Jeckyll. He was now asked to re-examine the building and alter any plans as necessary.

Warehouses in Town Green, owned by the trust and currently rented to Cornelius Tipple, were also in dire need of attention. Some repairs were also necessary to Mr. Grisdale's house.

Land acquired by the Methodist Church

Rather than spend money they could ill afford, repairing the old warehouses on Town Green, the trustees decided to put them up for sale. The Bill of Sale described the property as an:

> *extensive range of ruined buildings covering a valuable site, now chiefly used as a coal store.*

In June 1870 they were purchased by John Robert Smith, on behalf of the Methodist Church, for £300. The old and dangerous buildings were demolished and a new church was built on the site. In September of the same year, John Robert Smith, who owned a grocer's and draper's shop in the town, sent his sons Frederick (10 ½) and William (9 ½) to join the school. He was later to become the first non-conformist member of the trustees.

A sketch of the old warehouses, with demolition about to begin.

Becket's Chapel

The state of Becket's Chapel, however, was worse than feared. Thomas Jeckyll submitted drawings of the chapel as it was in 1871, and his plans for its future development, to the town's authorities. As we can see, his plans were not accepted.

A tender for £705 from Richard Mayes was accepted in November 1871, but five months later the builder went bankrupt, and the trustees were forced to accept a higher cost, from Woodbine and Colman, of £860. The Rev. W. D. Daniel gave permission for the builders to use his garden, but was unwilling to sell his properties adjoining Becket's Chapel, namely the coach house and the loft above, to the trustees. However, he did make a gift of part of the loft over the old lock-up. To enable the repairs to be carried out, the Trustees then purchased the cottage, stable, buildings and land attached to the chapel on the other side, between Chapelgate Street and Town Green, which had been acquired by William Clarke. All these buildings were pulled down to allow access.

Contract

PARTICULAR

AND

CONDITIONS OF SALE

OF A

PIECE OF FREEHOLD

BUILDING GROUND,

Containing 50 Rods or thereabouts,

FRONTING

Towngreen Street, Wymondham.

Together with the Building known as

"THE OLD WAREHOUSE,"

And all the other Buildings and Building Material thereon, which will be

Offered for sale by Auction,

BY

MR. S. T. CANN,

AT THE

King's Head Inn, Wymondham,

ON

Friday, the 7th day of January, 1870,

At Four for Five o'clock in the Afternoon.

F. J. HOWLETT,
VENDORS' SOLICITOR.

J. R. FORSTER, PRINTER, WYMONDHAM.

Particulars of the old warehouse in Town Green bought for the Methodist Church and -

The church built on the site.

Work on Becket's Chapel progressed slowly. In May 1873 it was still behind schedule. Although funds were very tight, the trustees and Mr. Grisdale refused the application of the twelve-year-old son of Mr. Daniels' coachman to attend the school. The only reason seems to have been one of class distinction.

Thomas Jeckyll's plan for the future, submitted in 1871

The chapel as it was in 1871.

In January 1875, the trustees lost patience with the progress of the Chapel repairs, and wrote to the contractors stating that they must be completed by March of that year. Iron railings were provided on the east and south sides of the Chapel, and it was used for its first function in September 1875 by the Independent Fairland Church. Mr. Glasspole, a local organ builder, offered to construct an organ in Becket's Chapel the next year, but his offer was refused. No doubt there was some measure of cost involved.

An unusual situation – a headmaster who wants to stay

It is clear that by this time the trustees were concerned about the continuation of Grisdale's tenure of office. He, like many other headmasters at this time, had no independent means, and therefore no income if he retired from his post. In September 1877, when he was 74, they put pressure on him by formally requesting him to give a six- monthly report on the school and its progress. These reports did not have the effect the trustees had hoped for, and were very brief, running to only a few lines. The number of pupils had by now reduced to 14, with only one boarder, and so the fact that Grisdale reported that the pupils were 'well-behaved' was only to be expected.

Change in Scholarships

The Endowed Schools Act of 1869 was to have many repercussions in Wymondham, although these did not appear immediately. It was not until 1881 that the Queen in Council approved the recommendation that there should be no more awards of the two fellowships at Norwich founded by Archbishop Parker in 1569, nor of either of the two scholarships founded by him with preference to scholars from Norwich, Wymondham or Aylsham Schools. All the money which had been used to pay for these in the past were now to maintain one Exhibition to Corpus Christi College, the candidates for which could be nominated from any of the three schools. Exhibitions to Corpus Christi, which had been founded later by Edward Colman, were untouched by these schemes. There continued to be apprehension in Wymondham regarding the choice between pupils from Norwich and Wymondham Schools, especially as the selection continued to be made in Norwich.

The 1870 Education Act

This Act made provision for board schools to be constructed for children under thirteen. Parents were to pay fees for their children's attendance, unless they were too poor to do so. It was only after 1891, when fees were abolished, that Wymondham Grammar School became open to competition.

Retirement of Grisdale

In December 1881 the governors were ready to put more pressure on Grisdale, and the Clerk was asked to ascertain his views about retiring. There were now only nine pupils in the school. Grisdale had now reached the age of 78 and been in the post for nearly forty years. He demanded a pension of £60 p.a. to retire, pointing out that he had been awarded a pension of £20 from his comparatively minor office of chaplain to the Bridewell Prison. The trustees hastily agreed to this request, but the Charity Commissioners would not consent to any more than a £50 p.a. pension.

The school was to find this sum a terrible burden on its finances, as it would have to pay the cost equivalent to almost twice the usual annual salary of the headmaster, without any additional income.

The trustees faced further disappointment when they discovered that the date set for Grisdale's retirement was not until September 1884. By this time he would be over 80 years old, and it soon became clear that the school could not really afford this quite-generous pension, which was paid for the next ten years. By 1884, the number of pupils had decreased to six, and subsequently to two before the arrival of Grisdale's successor. His advancing years could not have encouraged recruitment.

Should a headmaster still be a clergyman?

Earlier in June of that year, the trustees had started meeting in the clerk's office, rather than the King's Head, and it was here that decisions were taken regarding the new appointment. The trustees generally felt that the clause used previously, suggesting that candidates must be in Holy Orders, should be omitted from the candidates' requirements on this occasion, but the vicar, the Rev Eden, felt strongly that it should remain, and so it did.

The advertisement read,

> *Head master, a clergyman of the Church of England and graduate of Oxford or Cambridge required for the above school. Salary £60 p.a. and capitation fees with schoolhouse (capable of accommodating 30 boarders) garden and playground rent free. Subject to any provision established under the Endowed Schools Acts. Applications by 15th Dec.*

It was to appear in *The Guardian*, the *Norfolk Chronicle*, the *Norwich Mercury* and the *Lynn Advertiser*. On reading this, many locals from Wymondham wrote to the trustees, deploring the necessity for the applicant to be in Holy Orders.

The Earl of Kimberley advocated a new advert to read, 'not necessarily in Holy Orders', but his proposition was not carried, as applications had been received from eleven men who were in holy orders and from only five who were not.

Chapter 6

The last two headmasters 1884 - 1903

New headmaster

The trustees decided on the appointment of the Rev. Arthur W. Callis, on the condition that he made proper provision for French, Chemistry and Natural Science. He was a young man of thirty-one when he accepted the post, and must have seen the very low number of pupils as a challenge. He had just become ordained, and his experience as an assistant master, at what is now Cranleigh School, would have given him very useful experience. Numbers increased under him, and his enthusiasm led him to make innovations in building and repairs that it seems the school could ill afford. Occasionally he paid bills himself, and then claimed the sums back from the governors.

Visiting Bishop of Norwich

Callis set about his task with great enthusiasm. His previous contact with the Bishop of Norwich proved very useful, and the Bishop agreed to become a Visitor of the school. The trustees were delighted to have his name on the school prospectus, and were ready to help the new headmaster as far as funds would allow. Furniture had become rather sparse in the previous regime, and not replaced in view of the low number of pupils, and so it was agreed to immediately purchase desks for 32 boys and a master's desk and chair.

Further Innovations

In February 1885 Callis devised a new entrance exam. Out of 15 applications, twelve scholars, the agreed maximum, were admitted on the Foundation, at reduced fees. A blackboard, easel and maps were purchased. In the same year, in an attempt to bring the facilities of the school up to date, Callis requested, and was given permission to have, a Fives Court, if he could raise the necessary funding. More building repairs were considered. In fact, at every trustees' meeting, the headmaster came with a list of necessary building improvements and additions.

In January 1886, the governors were compelled to discuss a scheme devised for the Town Lands by the Charity Commissioners, in accordance with the 1869 Endowed Schools Act and subsequent Amending Acts. This was an extensive document, and suggested many alterations to the running of the school which were not all to the liking of many Wymondham people, including the headmaster, Mr. Callis, and the governors.

EXAMINER'S REPORT.

"In the brief period during which Mr. Callis has had charge of the School, the boys have done a very creditable amount of work.

"The tone is very good, and the boys seem imbued with a spirit for work.

"In the paper work on Latin, Grammar, and Arithmetic the boys have done well, especially those in the higher form. Smith gained full marks, both in Latin and Arithmetic, and is closely followed by Barnes, Owles, and Gotts.

"In the *vivâ voce* examination in History, Geography, and Holy Scripture, the boys answered eagerly and intelligently.

"The impression made upon me by the examination of the School is that the present condition of the School is one full of promise and encouragement.

"(Signed) THOS. ARCHBOLD, M.A.,
"Principal of the Diocesan Training College, Norwich."

"July 24th, 1885."

Inspection Report 1885, not long after Callis' arrival.

Charity Commissioners' suggestions

This document suggested that all the charities within the parish, including the school, were to be administered by the eleven governors as a single foundation under the name of Wymondham Grammar School Foundation. One third of the total income was to be used for apprenticing the poor children of the parish, in respect of the wishes and gifts of Robert Dey, and donations to the poor of Suton from the revenue of Blythe's Meadow. Any residue from this one third was to be spent providing coals for the needy of the parish. The remaining two-thirds of the revenue was to be used for educational purposes.

Governors' meetings had to take place at least twice a year, in Wymondham, and members were responsible for electing their own chairman. The Charity Commissioners were responsible for overseeing the accounts, and acknowledged that the pension of £50 per year, which had been granted to the Rev. Joseph Grisdale, should continue to be paid.

Holy Orders and graduation no longer compulsory

Headmasters were no longer required to be graduates of a university if they had other suitable qualifications recognised by the governors and the Charity Commissioners. They were allowed to be in Holy Orders, but this was no longer compulsory, and the regulations clearly stipulated they were not allowed to hold any benefice 'having the cure of souls', or undertake additional employment, without the governors' consent.

They were, however, given a free hand in the whole internal management of the school. It was stipulated that they should live in the school house and receive a salary of £60 p.a., to rise to £100 as soon as income would allow. From the tuition fee income of £4-£8 p.a., a capitation grant of £2-£3 per pupil p.a. was also to be paid to the headmaster. Payment for boarders was not to be more than £35 p.a.

All pupils were to pay fees, apart from those boys qualifying for the newly proposed Foundation Scholarships by having attended an elementary school in the Wymondham school district. These were limited to one per ten paying pupils, and at the time, with only 20 pupils in the school, would have been just two. The withdrawal of previous awards was likely to lead to a further reduction in the number of pupils.

Proposed Curriculum

The curriculum was defined to include geography, history, mathematics, Latin, at least one modern foreign language, natural science, drawing, drill and 'vocal music', as well as religious instruction and reading, writing, arithmetic, English grammar, composition and literature.

Age range

The definition, by the Charity Commission, of the age range of the pupils as being between 8 and 16, possibly rising to 17 with permission, brought an immediate response from Mr. Callis, who pointed out that the scholarships given by Archbishop Parker and Mr. Coleman could no longer be used, under these regulations, and that it would not be practicable for boys to enter Oxford or Cambridge. He also considered the inability of masters to charge for the teaching of private pupils to be unfair, and that the adoption of the scheme as outlined by the Charity Commissioners would put him at a financial disadvantage.

Condition of buildings

The report suggested that the buildings were in reasonable order and suitable for their purposes, but Mr. Callis pointed out many defects in a letter to the governors, perhaps the most important being the lack of a lavatory for the boys' use, the situation of the closets 'dangerously near the large schoolroom' and the lack of a pantry or larder in which cooked or uncooked food could be safely kept.

Governors' reactions to proposals

Thus the Charity Commissioners' report was very wide-ranging, and gave headmaster and governors plenty to think about. Many discussions took place in the town, and the governors sent their reply to the Charity Commissioners in May 1886, listing their disagreements with the proposed Wymondham scheme. They felt that the allocation of finance for non-educational purposes was too large. They wished to continue their present scheme of the election of two JPs and four representative governors by the assembled vestry of the parish of Wymondham. They initially wanted the clause regarding the provision for the headmaster to be in holy orders to remain, but later consented to its withdrawal.

They suggested that the headmaster should be allowed to take private pupils if it were not to the detriment of the school, and that water, coals and cleaning should be paid for out of expenses, as at Hingham, and not by the headmaster. The capitation fee was considered to be too low for the head's income, and the leaving age should be defined as 17, and up to 19, with head's consent. The reduction of the Foundation scholars was likely to cause much dissatisfaction among the inhabitants of Wymondham. All these concerns were forcibly expressed, but the reply to this letter took some time to appear, approximately one year.

The school at work

Meanwhile, the work of the school had continued. Callis introduced the idea of a Speech Day, which was held in the building now being known as 'Becket's Hall'. Repairs had already been started there, and, in spite of the many fears regarding the possible fall in pupil numbers, in September of 1886 Callis was requesting more desks for the 33 pupils now on the roll.

Repairs and redecorations continued, with a view to Becket's Chapel being used as the school once more. Two small stoves were installed, one at either end of the building, and the fireplace removed. Toilet facilities were provided, and also a place for hats and coats.

Fifteen shields, borne by persons or places closely connected with the town of Wymondham, were placed on the ceiling of the building, ready for its re-use in 1887, when the pupil numbers had increased to 41, with further additions likely. One of these was a fleur-de-lys, which was adopted as the school badge, and was placed over the entrance of all the school's buildings.

In the education department, the governors supported Callis' suggestion that there should be at least two teaching assistants, but the headmaster was probably not too pleased to be told that the total cost of these and all the school plant had to be less than £125 per annum. On a more positive note, he was to receive £5 per year for every boy in the school.

The 'fleur de lys' which was placed on the ceiling of Becket's Chapel.

Charity Commissioners' final decisions

In May 1887, the school received the final amendments to the Wymondham Town Lands Charities from the Charity Commissioners. It was as the draft, except that it was agreed that not as much as one third of its income should go to non-educational purposes, thereby limiting the sums from Dey's Charity for apprentices and the Blythe Meadow trust for the poor of Suton.

It reinforced the composition of new governors, previously suggested. Two were to be chosen by Norfolk JPs, acting in and for the Petty Sessional Division of Forehoe, two by the School Board of Wymondham, and two by the Vestry of Wymondham. The religious affiliation to the Church of England by the headmaster was no longer necessary.

All property was to be managed by the governors, who were empowered to dismiss the headmaster, if necessary, with 6 months' notice. Pupils were to leave at 17, unless special permission was given by the head and governors. The disputed £50 pension to Grisdale was to continue and be paid out of the foundation income. Masters were not to receive or demand any fee or payment except that authorised by the new scheme. The Head's salary was to be increased to £100 p.a., from £60, as soon as possible. He should also get a capitation payment of £2-£5 for each boy in the school.

Repairs on Becket's Chapel are about to begin. (The exact date of this photograph is unknown)

Scholarships
On the subject of scholarships, it was agreed that there could be five Foundation Scholars, with total exemption from fees if they had been in any of the public elementary schools in the school district of Wymondham. Other scholarships in the form of exemptions/partial exemptions were permissible at the rate of 1 for every 10 boys in the school. If there was enough money in hand, the governors could award exhibitions to places of advanced education for boys who had been in the school for at least 10 years.

Repairs
£500 of the 3% Government stock held was to be kept for repairs and renewals. Since the interest on this sum was less than £15 p.a. it must be made up from current income.

First Meeting under new scheme - parents informed of decisions
The implications of all the above directives were considered at the first meeting under the new scheme, held on 25th Aug 1887. Parents were made aware of the forthcoming changes, forced on the school, in a letter two months later. Tuition fees were to be £9 a year, but there would be a 10 shillings reduction per term for brothers. The governors were unable to continue the twelve existing foundation awards.

Rival schools founded
Responding very quickly to this depressing news to parents, George Hare published a circular stating that, because of the abolition of Foundation scholars at the Grammar School, he intended to organise a Middle Class school at The Rothbury to:

> *secure to the sons of tradesmen and others a sound commercial education at a minimum cost*

He offered a wide curriculum, including Latin, and the fees were very competitive at £6 per annum, with a reduction to £4 for brothers. He also offered boarding facilities for a limited number of pupils.

Parents' concerns
There was much communication in the press at this time, and letters from disgruntled Grammar School parents reached such a point in January 1888 that the governors felt they had to respond by writing to the EDP, pointing out that 12 boys had been educated as Foundation Scholars, paying reduced fees of £6 per annum, but against their wishes the Charity Commissioners had insisted that all reductions in fees were abolished. One parent had even pointed out that

The new Commercial School was housed in 'The Rothbury', on the corner of Rothbury Road and Pople Street.

a former master (Grisdale) was still in receipt of a pension to the detriment of the school's finances.

The governors at this time (1888) were The Earl of Kimberley, Chairman, Canon W. Eden, the Rev. W. D. Daniel, William Cann, J.P., E Beeston, H. Edwards, J.P., E. Routh Clarke, E Pomeroy, W. Fryer, G. Plumstead, V. Jermyn.

Further competition

At the same time, in another attempt to remedy the educational provision in the town, following the withdrawal of Foundation Scholars, Edward Allen advertised that he would be opening a commercial school on Jan 13th 1888. The fees for this would be only 6 guineas per annum, and provision for boarders was likely to be made.

Callis buys York House

In March 1888, the house, which Callis and his wife had been renting for £20 per year, came up for sale. It was described as having various outbuildings, some of which were used by the pupils of Wymondham Grammar School as a gymnasium and a workshop. Callis decided to purchase the house himself if possible, and he was indeed successful, at the auction on March 23rd, for the

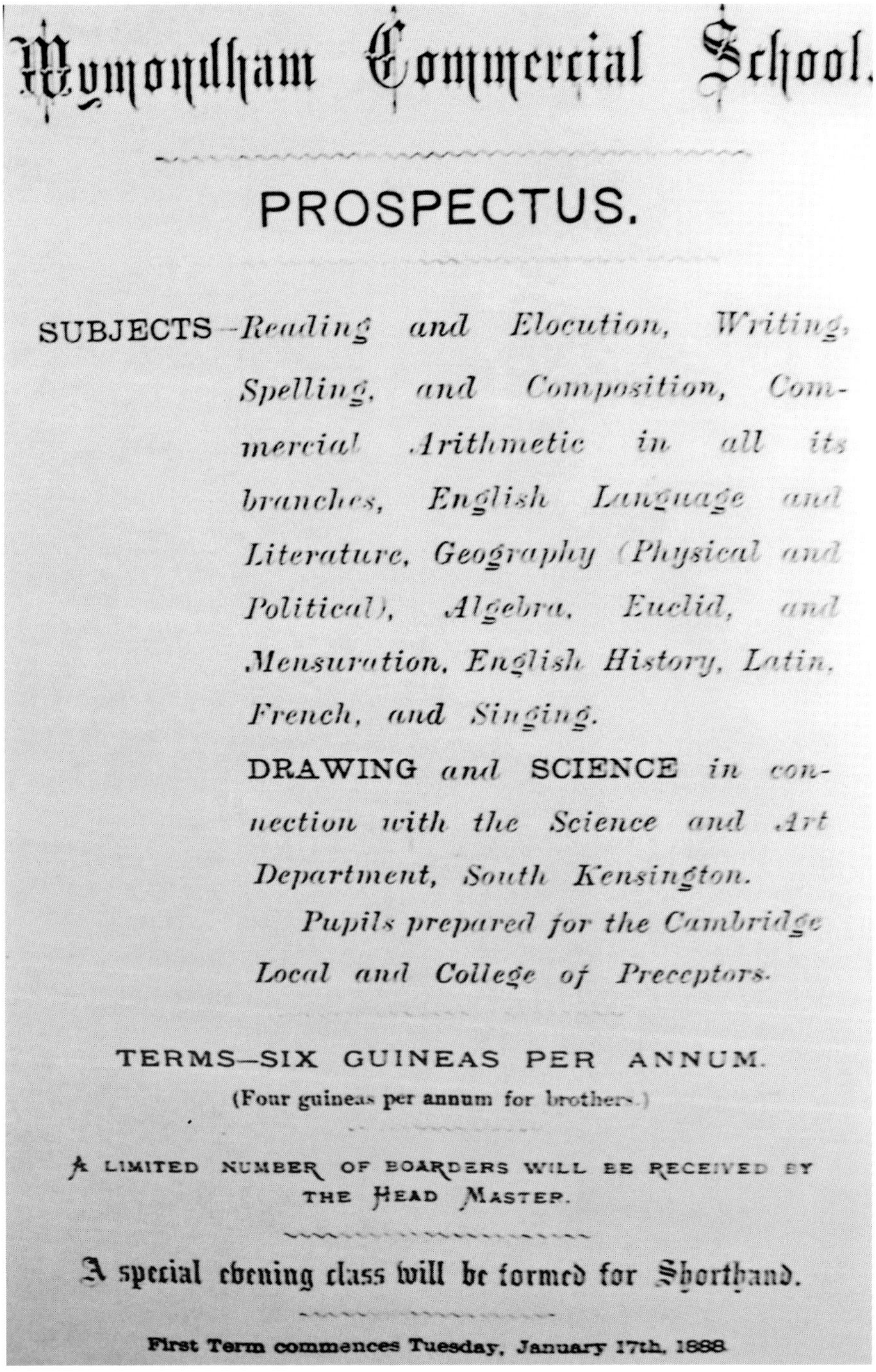

Wymondham Commercial School.

PROSPECTUS.

SUBJECTS—*Reading and Elocution, Writing, Spelling, and Composition, Commercial Arithmetic in all its branches, English Language and Literature, Geography (Physical and Political), Algebra, Euclid, and Mensuration, English History, Latin, French, and Singing.*

DRAWING *and* **SCIENCE** *in connection with the Science and Art Department, South Kensington.*

Pupils prepared for the Cambridge Local and College of Preceptors.

TERMS—SIX GUINEAS PER ANNUM.

(Four guineas per annum for brothers.)

A LIMITED NUMBER OF BOARDERS WILL BE RECEIVED BY THE HEAD MASTER.

A special evening class will be formed for Shorthand.

First Term commences Tuesday, January 17th, 1888

Prospectus for George Hare's commercial school

Four pages from the 1888 Prospectus

King Edward VI. Grammar School.

WYMONDHAM, NORFOLK.

FOUNDED A.D. 1551.

DIEU ET MON DROIT

HONI SOIT QUI MAL Y PENSE

Visitor:

THE HON. AND RIGHT REV.
THE LORD BISHOP OF NORWICH.

Governors:

THE RT. HON. THE EARL OF KIMBERLEY, K.G., *Chairman.*

THE REV. CANON EDEN, M.A.	H. W. B. EDWARDS, ESQ., J.P.
THE REV. W. D. DANIEL, M.A.	E. ROUTH CLARKE, ESQ.
WILLIAM CANN, ESQ., J.P.	E. B. POMEROY, ESQ.
E. BEESTON, ESQ.	W. B. FRYER, ESQ.
	MR. G. PLUMSTEAD.
	MR. V. JERMYN.

F. J. HOWLETT, ESQ., *Clerk to the Governors.*

Head Master:

REV. A. W. CALLIS, M.A., ST. JOHN'S COLLEGE, CAMBRIDGE.

Second Master:

MR. F. ROSENBERG, B.A.,
SCHOLAR OF EMMANUEL COLLEGE, CAMBRIDGE (16th Wrangler, 1886).

Assistant Masters:

MR. G. W. DOIDGE, LON. UNIV.
MR. R. COCHRANE, *Drawing.*
MR. J. A. HARCOURT, *Music.*

FORM.	*Scripture.*	*Latin.*	*French.*	*History.*	*Geography.*	*English.*	*Science.*	*Mathematic*
IV.	Genesis. Exodus. St. Luke.	Virgil, Æn. VII. Grammar. Composition Unseen Translation.	Bonnechose Lazare Hoche. Composition	1603 to 1689.	Africa. Great Britain and Dependencies.	Shakespere's "Tempest."	Roscoe's "Chemistry"	Arithmetic. Euclid, I to I Algebra. Mechanics.
III.	Ditto.	Virgil, Æn. VII. Henry. Primer.	Ditto.	Ditto.	Great Britain and Dependencies.	Ditto.	Ditto.	Arithmetic. Euclid I. Algebra.
II.	St. Luke.	Cæsar. Helvetian War. Grammar. Exercises.	Grammar and Exercises.	1485 to 1603.	Europe.	Macaulay's "Horatius."	Bert's "Scientific Knowledge."	Arithmetic.
I.	Ditto.	Accidence and Exercises.	Ditto.	Dates and Outlines.	Great Britain.	Macaulay's "Armada" and "Ivry."	Ditto.	Ditto.

Work for next Term

MIDSUMMER ORDER.

(The Roman figures in brackets denote Mathematical Forms, the Arabic figures the positions in those Forms.)

Fourth Form.

1 Owles (iv. 1)
2 { Taylor ii. (iv. 3)
   Skinner (iv. 2)
4 Foulds (iv. 4)
5 Taylor i. (iv. 8)
6 Tomlins (iv. 9)
7 { Wells (iv. 14)
   Palmer i. (iv. 6)
9 Semmence i. (iii. 4)

Second Form.

1 Callis (iii. 13)
2 Skelton (ii. 3)
3 Sanders (iii. 7)
4 Thurston (iv. 9)
5 Tricker (iii. 3)
6 Sutton (iii. 9)
7 { Jackson (iii. 12)
   Rivett ii. (ii. 2)
9 Wainwright (ii. 6)
10 Rivett i. (iii. 8)
11 Smith iv. (iv. 12)
12 Sheppard (ii. 9)
13 { Silcock (ii. 8)
   Bagshaw i. (ii. 4)
15 Dring ii. (ii. 7)
16 Stanley (ii. 11)

Third Form.

1 Howlett i. (ii. 1)
2 Ringer (iv. 9)
3 Pomeroy (iv. 4)
4 Palmer ii. (iii. 1)
5 Clements i. (iii. 6)
6 Smith ii. (iii. 2)
7 Lane (iv. 7)
8 Bagshaw ii. (ii. 2)
9 Everitt (iii. 10)
10 Frankling (iii. 5)
11 { Hammond (iv. 13)
   Dring i. (iii. 14)
   Reynolds (iii. 11)
14 Bailey ii. (iii. 15)
15 Allen (ii. 6)
16 Barker i. (ii. 5)

First Form.

1 Bailey iii. (i. 1)
2 Semmence iii. (i. 1)
3 Howlett ii. (i. 6)
4 Smith iii. (i. 2)
5 Dring iii. (i. 4)
6 Clements iv. (i. 7)
7 Clements iii. (i. 3)
8 Barker ii. (ii. 10)
9 Peele (i. 5)
10 { Clements ii. (i. 8)
   Barker iii. (i. 9)

School Lists

sum of £335. This must have provided some encouragement for the unhappy parents.

Headmaster soldiers on

In spite of all these setbacks, Callis continued his work with unabated enthusiasm. The prizes presented at Speech Day that year were either donated by friends or by the head himself. The latter also seems to have paid visiting examiners to the school.

E. Pomeroy laying the foundation stone of the Public/Town Hall. November 1888. Note the Grammar School boys at the front.

More repairs necessary

The perennial requests for repairs and innovations were discussed. The headmaster complained that the kitchen range needed repair, the boiler was cracked, and the stable used for storing fuel had become dangerous – a servant had been injured when the floor of the loft gave way under him. He considered that the present building used as a gymnasium was too small for this purpose, and suggested the provision of one to be built in the playground, the one acre of open land across the road from Priory House, for the price of £60. The governors agreed to his setting up a fund to try and raise this sum.

More financial problems

Money continued to be in very short supply. In April 1889, Callis wrote to the Clerk of the Governors, politely requesting that an overdue cheque should be paid in to his account, as the funds there were very small. A few days later, he complained that Gurney's Bank had charged him £1 9s 10d because he had drawn out all the balance.

In 1889, the financial problems of the school became even more evident, as the income from land had not risen to the same degree as the school's costs. Callis wanted to repair the dining hall, but was told there was no money available. He was also asked to conduct the examinations for the Foundation scholars himself rather than employ an outside examiner. He was, however, given permission to offer two scholarships of £15 per annum, if he could arrange the funding. Correspondence of this period reveals that the cash flow was a constant problem, and there was often a wait for incoming cheques to be cleared before payments could be made.

Speech Day 1889

The headmaster's report, given to parents at Speech Day in August 1889, was more positive. The governors had insisted on seeing it prior to its delivery, in spite of Callis' request to the contrary. It revealed that the school had escaped a serious outbreak of measles in the town, and there had been successes in the Cambridge Local Examinations and all the others. The appeal for the gymnasium was going well, but progress in Science was limited as there was no laboratory for experiments. Once again, the prizes had been generously donated by friends of the school. It was probably not publicised that this was because there was insufficient money in the foundation funds.

School Policies

Some interesting details of school policies can be found from the prospectus of the school at this time. Fines were imposed for lateness. The cost was 2s 6d for the first day and 1s for each following day. All proceeds went to the expenses

The Rev. A.Callis with Junior boys outside Priory House. It is probably Mrs. Callis and an usher in the back row, and the Second Master seated.

of the school library and games. Regulation caps had to be worn. It was also reported that special arrangements could be made for boys from the colonies to join the school. The person to whom reference was to be made was C. Callis, the headmaster's brother, who lived in Wellington, New Zealand.

Changes in the early 1890s

By 1890, there were 50 boys in the school, and a precedent was made in the appointment of John Robert Smith, a leading Methodist, as a representative governor in place of E. Routh Clark. On October 15th of that year, Callis purchased the Cromer Coffee Tavern and Lecture Hall for £54, to use for the school's gymnasium. He had been forced to sign a legal document that he would be responsible for both its initial cost and its re-erection in the school playground.

The same spot in 2009.

A drawing of the Gymnasium and Fives Court, which appeared in the local paper in 1892

Memorial window

Again at their personal expense, Mr. and Mrs. Callis commissioned a window to be inserted into the south wall of the Chapel. This was in memory of their nephew, William Tinkler, who had been a pupil at the school from 1885 to 1890, and who had accidentally drowned.

Attempts to raise more money

To alleviate the poor financial situation, it was suggested that the tenants of the Grammar School lands should pay for the necessary drainage of their allotments. Unfortunately, they all refused to pay the suggested sums, but reluctantly agreed when the demands were considerably reduced. It was only after this that the necessary work could be undertaken.

In 1891 the number of pupils in the school fell to 43, and the fees were increased. The governors felt it imperative that they should tighten up, both financially and academically. One Foundation scholar, reported as being idle and unpunctual, was told in no uncertain terms that his scholarship would be removed if he failed to improve. The governors also agreed to carry out their threat to insist that boys leave the school if the arrears of their fees were not paid. On a more positive note, the new gymnasium was officially opened by the Chairman of Governors, the Earl of Kimberley. More than half of the cost had already been raised.

Headmaster investigates possibility of a laboratory

The problem of the lack of a laboratory for scientific experiments was brought to the attention of the governors. Correspondence at this time clearly reveals that one could be provided only with grants and donations. There was no money available from school funds. Repairs continued to be a drain on resources.

With characteristic enthusiasm, the headmaster began investigating ways in which the proposed laboratory could be provided. He maintained that there was no room or space in the present building to provide one, and suggested they use a detached room in part of the property he owned adjoining the school house. This was agreed, and negotiations began with the Technical Education Committee of Norfolk County Council to help fit up a laboratory for chemistry and physics. We can today still see the mock Tudor building used, next to York House.

Mr. Callis' contribution

It was agreed by the County Council that £75 should be given to Wymondham Grammar School on condition that Norfolk County Council Scholarships were offered at the school. Callis agreed to being responsible for paving the floor in the building which he had suggested could be used as a laboratory, for improving the lighting there and making any minor adjustments. In return, the governors agreed to pay him a rent of £5 per annum, and fund £42 for further apparatus and £6 17s for a tank and force pump. An extension to the curriculum was also agreed, and the headmaster was granted permission to hold science

The new laboratory. Notice the fleur-de-lys above the window.

and art classes, possibly with a government grant, but not to dispense with Latin.

Overdue fees continued to be a problem in 1892. By August, Callis had still not been paid his £60 annual salary, but it had been promised for when there were sufficient funds.

1893 – A better year

1893 brought some welcome good news. At Speech Day that year, when the writer and Norfolk farmer, Henry Rider Haggard, came to present the prizes, it was reported that three boys had gained scholarships of £50 per annum from Norfolk County Council, who offered a total of fifteen in the whole county, and R. H. McMullon had been awarded a Parker Scholarship, in competition with pupils from Norwich Grammar School. The debt on the gymnasium had been cleared, and there were now 65 boys in the school, eight of whom had learnt to swim at Wramplingham. The fact that the headmaster had at last received his stipend for the previous year was not reported to the public.

Financial problems return – headmaster resigns

The good news of 1893 was short-lived. In March 1894, Callis wrote to the governors saying the allocation of £125 for additional masters was insufficient, as, without their board, the cost was £210. As well as finding this shortfall, he was expected to pay taxes, for school repairs and for the coal, coke and gas used by the school. Unfortunately, although the governors were sympathetic to his situation, they were unable to offer much material help. In June of that year, it was with obvious disappointment that they subsequently received his resignation, to move to what must have been a similar but more prestigious school at Bury St. Edmunds. In their reply, they said that he had:

> *raised the school from the exceedingly low condition into which it had fallen to the present flourishing position it occupies among the Grammar Schools of the County.*

Another advertisement

In the advertisement for the vacant post of headmaster, an encouraging picture was painted. The salary was still to be £60 per annum, but with the additional benefit of a capitation fee of £5 per boy. Since the school boasted 63 boys at this time, including 28 boarders, this was, on the surface, an attractive salary. It became less so when it was discovered that Callis had managed to persuade twenty-four boarders to move to Bury with him. Although this move may appear a somewhat 'sharp practice' today, it was quite common for boys to move with their headmaster at this time.

A panoramic view of some of the school buildings. Between Priory House and the new laboratory is York House, which was owned by the Rev. Callis. Becket's Chapel was being used as the schoolroom.

Speech Day lunch. August 3rd 1892

The school in 1893, outside the gymnasium and fives court.

Appointment of new headmaster

In spite of the serious financial situation, the governors received more than fourteen applications for the vacant headmastership. Seven were selected for interview. The favourite, the Rev. A E Burton from York, was taken round the school by Mr. Callis, and offered the position. He declined to accept the post, stating in his reply, that, having been taken round the school by the present head,

> *I see no prospect of the school paying its way and affording a living wage to the Head Master for some years to come.*

The post was then offered to Mr. Burnside, who accepted by telegram on August 10th 1894.

Unfortunately, the potential loss of the use of Callis' private house meant that the school also lost its laboratory. Consequently the governors applied to the Charity Commission for permission to purchase the house at a cost of £490. This was not granted, and the trustees continued to pay Mr. Callis the £5 annual rent for the laboratory until the school closed in 1903.

More financial gloom

The fears expressed by Mr. Burton, on his tour of the school, were soon realised. In 1895 the governors were faced with a repayment bill from Mr. Callis of just

School teams in the 1890s.

Mr Callis and other masters played for these teams, and in 1889, Callis topped the batting averages. A very versatile sportsman, he also played for Wymondham Football Club.

The schoolroom, and an enlargement of one of the pillars on which the boys 'inscribed' their names.

under £100, for repairs he had commissioned while still in office, and others, including the salary of the clerk to the governors, of a further £45. Agricultural depression had reduced rents, and some were unpaid. With no possible means of finding such sums, the governors applied to the Charity Commissioners to draw £150 of their £700 of Consols stock. This was reluctantly allowed, but the terms were harsh.

The money had to be paid back in ten years, and the Charity Commissioners ensured that this happened by allowing no further interest on the foundation's stock to be paid until the £150 had been paid off. Thus income was depleted, which exacerbated the already tricky financial situation. Cost cutting measures were necessary. In response to falling numbers of pupils, the allocation for assistant masters' salaries was reduced from a total of £125 to £75 for 1895 and future years.

In January 1896 the governors, investigating other possible sources of income, claimed a portion of the Wymondham Hendry Charity. Unfortunately the deeds of 1724 relating to this bequest had gone missing, and therefore further investigations were necessary before any money could be obtained.

New headmaster's plans

Meanwhile Mr. Burnside was continually requesting repairs and improvements to the fabric of the buildings. The outside of the school needed painting, the roof was unsafe and the drains in the schoolyard were continually blocked. He pointed out that prospective parents were put off by the appearance of the buildings, and that they had commented to him that the school charged higher fees than its rivals, but provided fewer benefits.

Governors try to raise more money

In an attempt to inject more cash into the school, the governors looked to another charity, this time the Blythe Charity. This was a perfectly reasonable approach, since the income for it also came from the revenues of the Town Lands. Unfortunately the sum eventually received was only £7 6s 0d, which did not make much impact on the school's finances.

From October 1896 the governors began to meet annually, while the number of pupils continued to decline. A possible reduction of fees from £9 to £6 per term was discussed, but it was agreed that, although the governors would like to see this, it was not possible. There was still a long list of repairs to be completed, but only the most essential were sanctioned. In May 1899, an embarrassing situation arose for Mr. Burnside, when he was invited to take the school's cricket team for a match against Bury St. Edmunds Grammar School, where Mr. Callis continued to maintain a very successful and flourishing school.

Matters go from bad to worse

Financial matters continued to dominate the governors' agenda. With a continuous decrease in numbers, in 1901, Mr. Burnside, becoming more desperate, suggested that the governors should apply to the Norfolk County Council for financial help, as other schools had received grants in similar circumstances. He said that the boarding facilities needed considerable improvements to bring them up to the standards of similar schools. Advice was also sought from Mr. Dufton, a visiting school inspector. His response was to send the governors the prospectuses of some mixed schools, which he described as great successes. However, there is no evidence that the governors followed his advice and considered taking girls as pupils.

Financial report of 1901

In June 1901 the governors made a full report of finances. It had become necessary to spend approximately £50 for providing a cold water supply, fixing two baths and four lavatories in the schoolhouse, and heating apparatus, including a boiler, in Becket's Chapel.

Many ways of reducing fees, saving money and attracting more pupils were discussed. They included turning Becket's Chapel into two classrooms and the school being made a School of Science under the Board of Education. This would mean a grant of 50 shillings for each pupil. Unfortunately, it would involve much expense in bringing the buildings up to an accepted standard as well as providing bathrooms in the dormitories. It would be necessary to apply to the Charity Commission to release at least £500 of the £624 consols stock remaining, if these repairs were to be carried out. Another suggestion was to apply to Norfolk Technical Education Committee for a contribution towards the cost of employing a technical master and/or an allowance towards the building of a laboratory.

Decisions taken

A decision to reduce the fees to £6 per annum and the capitation fees to £4 per pupil was taken, although the latter depended upon the number of pupils reaching 40. Income was still a crucial factor in this, and there had been further difficulty in renting all the Town Lands.

The school in 1902

The financial outlook remained dire, but the school did receive a grant of £11 15s 4d for technical education for the Autumn Term from the Norfolk County Council.

Burnside 'soldiers on'

In spite of all the problems, the work of the school continued to the best of the staff's abilities. The report from the Inspector of Maths and Science from the Cambridge Syndicate, the Rev. F. R. Tennant, MA, said that the standard of pupils' work was 'generally as satisfactory as one could reasonably expect'. At this point there were 22 boys in the school. A breakdown in numbers reveals that there were 3 boys in Form 5, 3 boys in Form 4, 8 boys in Forms 2 and 3 combined, and 8 boys in Form 1. One pupil in Form 5, Hanworth, had done very well. He was also commended in the report from the Rev. J. R. Wilson, MA, of Jesus College, Cambridge, who inspected most subjects.

Death of the Earl of Kimberley 1902

The school was very sorry to learn of the death of its Chairman of Governors, the Earl of Kimberley, at this time. He had the distinction of holding the post of Colonial Secretary in Gladstone's government of 1870, but always found time to honour his local responsibilities and act as chairman at governors' meetings. He later became Chairman of Norfolk Education Committee, and was able to use his experience to the benefit of Wymondham Grammar School. Unfortunately, he was not able to add to the school's endowments.

Mr. Burnside resigns

In September of that year Mr. Burnside offered his resignation for December 1902. His letter stated that the immediate reason was the withholding of capitation fees by the governors. News of Mr. Burnside's resignation spread fast, and an application was received from J. Watson of Bognor Regis. However, the governors managed to persuade Mr. Burnside to continue until Easter 1903, while they considered the type of headmaster they required.

Appointment of a successor

The clauses in the original foundation documents that headmasters should hold a degree from Cambridge or Oxford did not seem practical in view of the reduced status and circumstances of the school, and one governor, Mr. Lee Warner, suggested that a trained elementary school teacher would be more suitable, but the Board of Education replied that a special case could not be made for Wymondham. It implied that the school wanted to appoint a headmaster who was not properly qualified.

Closure of the school?

At the end of 1902, the governors requested the maximum grant from the Board of Education, outlining their plans for further improvements to the school, including new classrooms on the meadow opposite School House, costing approximately £1000, of which they had only £125, and that was provided the

Charity Commissioners would release this sum. This request must have fallen upon deaf ears, as in January 1903 it was made again, this time pointing out that the number of pupils had fallen to twenty-one and the fees had been reduced from £9 to £6 per term. Debts of £188 had also been incurred, and the governors sought advice as to whether the school should continue. It was agreed that they should meet a member of the Board of Education and discuss this issue before the school advertised for another head.

Last attempts to save the school

Burnside left the school in March 1903, but was allowed to stay in the schoolhouse until December, at a rent of £1 per month and payment of rates. The appointment of another headmaster was considered, but it was not clear what sort of person was required. There were many changes in education nationally at this time.

The Board of Education's inspector, Mr. Mitcheson, came to Wymondham to discuss the unsatisfactory nature of the school's finances, and at the next governors' meeting, it was proposed by Rev. the Hon. A. Parker, and seconded by Mr. F. W. Standley (Parish Councillor representative) that the school be closed and the funds diverted to a new scheme. It was requested that £150 should be drawn from the remaining monies to pay off the headmaster, and to meet other liabilities.

The governors did not give up without considering all possible alternatives to closure. An offer of help was made to the governors by Gurney's Bank, in the form of a loan of £100, but this was too small a sum to deal with the problem. Other avenues were also explored. All the Town Lands were inspected to see if any trees could be felled to raise money for necessary repairs to the School House, and the sale of one piece of land, known as Lot 12, which had always been difficult to let, was also considered.

In June 1903, as a result of Mr. Mitcheson's visit, the Endowment received a letter from the Board of Education saying that the resources of Wymondham Grammar School were insufficient to maintain it. The governors had little chance of reversing this decision, but were told that, if they could provide the necessary funds, then closure would be reconsidered. Unfortunately those funds could not be found.

Post Mortem

There have been several attempts to analyse the circumstances and events which led to the school's closure. It appears to have been due to a number of events beyond the control of the trustees.

First of all, Churchgate House was the only additional endowment to the original lands and properties which established the school in 1561. The income from these lands varied with the economic prosperity of the country as a whole, and aggregate rents generally deteriorated, particularly during the period from 1880 until the end of the century. There was little the trustees could do about this. They could only pay the wages and the maintenance bills as and when their income allowed. The very small number of pupils at the end of Joseph Grisdale's period of office, together with the £50 annual pension awarded to him by the Charity Commission for nearly ten years, exacerbated the situation. Arthur Callis came full of enthusiasm and suggestions to improve the school. He rapidly increased the pupil numbers, but the lack of funds limited the completion of many of his innovative ideas.

Rival Schools

Other schools, both private and national, were established in Wymondham during the nineteenth century. The Rev. William Papillon, Vicar of Wymondham, provided two national schools in the town, and by 1834 about 200 children were receiving a basic education. Other schools were founded, in the Fairland and on Norwich Common. In 1872 the Wymondham School Board

The former schoolhouse at Hingham. (By kind permission of Mrs. J. Lys)

was established, and took over the lease of the school on Norwich Common to provide education for 50 children. The Browick Road Schools were built in 1876 to accommodate 360 boys and girls.

However, the school which probably made the most impact on pupil numbers at the Grammar School was the Commercial School, which advertised boarding facilities, and very competitive fees. As already stated, this was established by George Hare in 1886, and advertised itself as catering for the middle classes. Although it closed in 1898, at one stage it is reported as having 100 pupils.

Grammar schools in other parts of Norfolk had also experienced difficulties. In Aylsham, the school, founded in 1517 by Robert Jennys, again with a small endowment, had ceased to be independent, and joined the National system by 1829. The school at Scarning, founded in 1638, by the will of William Seckar, changed its status in 1819, when an investigation into its endowment revealed that the money had been left for the poor of the village and not for the rich. It then became a free school for children over five.

The neighbouring rival school at Hingham, founded in 1727 on land conveyed under the will of William Partlett to Sir John Wodehouse and others, seems to have fared little better. It faced the same financial problems confronting the Wymondham governors, although it too had kept up-to-date with the introduction of science into the curriculum. Closure was discussed in 1906 although the school battled on until the end of 1908. An interesting footnote is that in 1893, with approximately 27 pupils, Hingham School had been unable to match the football talents of its Wymondham counterpart, losing both matches played that year.

Becket's Chapel in the 1930's.

Post Closure - Key Facts

In 1903 Becket's Chapel was closed for 20 years, after which time it was cleaned and then used for town functions.

By 1907, the debts of the school had been cleared, and the income of the endowment was once more in excess of its expenditure.

In 1912 the governors, considering proposals from the Board of Education, and anxious to use their income for its intended purposes, decided to use one-half of its income to provide Exhibitions, tenable at nearby recognised Secondary Schools, for Wymondham children. These awards resulted in the payment of all tuition fees at these schools. The other half of the income was to be spent on maintenance grants to pupils of the town, whether or not they had obtained an Exhibition.

In the same year, repairs were necessary to the Lizard cottage and the Grammar School house, after the Wymondham flood.

In 1913 the new title of the foundation became - Wymondham Old Grammar School Endowment.

In 1922, 13 scholars (boys and girls) were receiving £10 per year in grants

In 1930, negotiations began to move the library from the Market Cross to Becket's Chapel. At this time, it was run by volunteers, with books loaned from the County Library.

HM Office of Works made an application to purchase land opposite Priory House, as the site for a new Post Office. (1934) The tenant, Colonel Prior, agreed to this, after negotiations, and the sale proceeded. In 1939, a piece of land adjoining the above site was also sold to the Post Office.

In 1940, £25 was paid by the military authorities for damages which had been caused by an army lorry to the wall and gatepost on the remaining piece of Endowment land opposite Priory House.

In 1948, the Library became an official branch of the County Library, with a professional librarian and paid staff.

The headmaster's house and former school, Priory House, was eventually sold on May 7th 1954.

In the early 1990s, the William Tinkler memorial window, together with all the coloured glass throughout the building, was removed.

In 2008 the County Library moved from Becket's Chapel to its purpose-built premises in Back Lane.

The Post Office and the remaining school lands (Priory Gardens) in the 1940s

The Grammar School Foundation continues to award grants to senior-school pupils and university students.

Headmasters of Wymondham Grammar School

App	Left	Surname	First Name	OtherAppointm.	Special ref.	Salary
1574?	1584?	James				
?1584	1589	Leverington	Thomas		surgeon	
1589	1590?	Corbald	Thomas	author	author	£15 p.a.
1590?	1603	Wells	Simon	Vicar 1590-1603		£15 p.a.
1603	1606	Leverington	Thomas	priest	son of above	£15 p.a.
1606	1609?	Gary				£15 p.a.
1609	1609	Castleton	Henry?		pd. for 1/4 only	£15 p.a.
1609	1614	Easton	Nicholas	schoolmaster		£20 p.a.
1615	1616?	Browne			v. little info	£20 p.a.
1616	1618	Firmory				
1618	1619	Peacham	Henry	author/artist		£20 p.a.
1619	1621	Cudworth			v. little info	£20 p.a.
1621	1627	Gibbon	John			£20 p.a.
1627	1640	Locke	William	Rect Bunwell		£20 p.a.
1640	1643	Wildman	Francis?		Mr. Door usher?	£20 p.a.
1644?	1647	Mathews	William	priest	died in harness	£20 p.a.
1647	1650	Firmary	John	priest	Mr. English usher?	£20 p.a.
1651	1653	Bradford	Thomas	priest/master	Mr. English usher?	£25?p.a.
1653	1660	Ransome	Richard	Rector Nfk		£20 p.a.
1660	1660	Jermy	Anthony	Rector Nfk	stayed 6 months	£10
1660	1662	Callard	Robert		s. of Rect.Wramp	£20 p.a.
1662	1668	Tyrrell	Henry			£20 p.a.
1668	1672	Morphew	John	curate Wym	d. from smallpox	£20 p.a.
1672	1707	Clarke	Richard	curate Wym?		£20 p.a.
1707	1712	Taylor	George	Vicar Wym		
1709	4wks	Purt	Mark	Curate Wym	moved away	£30p.a
1713	1721	Sayer	Isaac	Curate?Wym	d at 36	£20 p.a.
1721	1735	Brett	Joseph	Rect Kimberley	cruel?	£20 p.a.
1735	1755	Evans	William		died in harness	£20 p.a.
1757	1757	Matthew	Frederick		d. mental probs.	£20 p.a.
1758	1768	Langham	Thomas	curate	memor. in church	£20 p.a.

Appo inted	Left	Surname	First Name	OtherAppointm.	Special ref.	Salary
1770	1778	Hepworth	Joseph	teacher	ret. to N Walsh.	£20 p.a.
1778	1788	Taylor	Thomas	Rect Nfk	refused house	£20 p.a.
1790	1817	Buston	Roger	Curate/Rect Nfk	refused house	£30 p.a.
1818	1819	Raven	John H.	new priest		
1825	1830	Kidd	Thomas	priest	50+, wife	60 gu
1830	1830	Cubitt	James	Rect		60 gu
1830	1838	Kirby	Richard		left suddenly - ill	60 gu
1841	1842	Slipper	Robert B.		v. socially aware	60 gu
1844	1884	Grisdale	Joseph	Norwich	went on to 78	60 gu
1884	1894	Callis	Arthur	priest		60 gu
1894	1903	Burnside	John W.			60 gu +

Some dates cannot be confirmed. The gaps represent a period when the school was closed because no master could be appointed.

A classroom scene in the 1890's. Roland Palmer, who had been football captain as a pupil, now appears to be an usher/master.

Wymondham Grammar School Pupils

Surname	First name	Father	Home area	Entry Univ	Later position
*brothers					
Jewel	George	John	Scoulton	1565	
Dove	Richard	Henry	Attleborough	1569	Church
Cattelyne	Ralph	Richard (gent)	b. in London	1572	Church
Randell	William	Robert	b. Carlton Rode	1582	Church
Welles	Robert	Thomas (yeoman)	b. Gissing	1584	Lect. @ Gonv. and Caius
Wish	Thomas	John (mf)	b. Norwich	1585	
Coppin	Joel	George Rect.of	Besthorpe	1595	
Dickerson	Nicholas	Nicholas - yeoman	Wymondham	1600	Mast Bury St Ed
Bucke	Richard	Edmund	Wymondham	1600	
Spendlove	John	Henry (gent)	b. Wroxham	1602	Church
Dey	Oliver	Robert-yeoman	Wymondham	1603	Church
*Castleton	Henry	John - gent	Wymondham	1603	Church
Le Groos	Charles (heir)	Thomas (knight)	Crostwight Nfk	1611	law & MP 1640
Neve	Richard	Robert Rect of	Swanton Morley	1611	Church
Mundeford	Edmund	Edmund (Knight)	Mundford	1612	MP in LongParl
Cotton	Francis	Roger (carpenter)	Wramplingham	1612	Mast at Roydon/
Wetherall	Robert	Robert	Wymondham	1613	Church
Atkins	Simon	Thomas	Barney, Nfk	1614	Church
Bretton	John	John (vicar)	Gt. Dunham	1614	Church
*Castleton	Martin	John (attorney)	Wymondham	1616	Church
Freeman	Thomas	Isaiah	Wymondham	1618	Church
Duffield	John	John (draper)	Wymondham	1621	
Caly	John	William yeoman	Salhouse	1631	Church
Burrell	Anthony	William	Wymondham	1633	Church
Rous	Thomas	Edward (clerk)	Flordon	1637	Church
Scott	Christopher	Robert (gent)	Letton	1639	
Barnard	Edmund	John (gent)	Wymondham	1639	Church
Kett	Esau	Stephen - butcher	Wymondham	1640	Church
Bayes	Robert	Thomas (husbandman)	Kimberley	1640	Church
Tailor	Thomas	Stephen (gent)	Kimberley	1641	Church/master
Wetherall	Robert	Robert (clerk)	Hethel	1643	
Bunning	John	Richard (gent)	Denton Nfk	1643	
Rogerson	Robert	Thomas	Norton Nfk	1645	Church
Seaman	William	Thomas (doctor)	Wymondham	1647	travel+ambass. Turkey

Surname	First name	Father	Home area	Entry Univ	Later position
*brothers					
Reeve	Henry	Augustin (gent)	Bracondale	1658	Grays Inn
Le Neve	Francis	Henry (gent)	Witchingham	1659	Grays Inn
Proctor	William	Francis(butcher)	Wymondham	1662	Cur Wym
Joyner	William	Robert (druggist)	Hingham	1674	
Jubbes	Martin	John (gent)	Wymondham	1679	Lincoln's Inn
Lawes	Peter	Stephen (brewer)	Carlton Rode	1680	church/master Aylsham
Rant	Humphrey	Humphrey (gent)	Yelverton	1681	
*Gurdon	Thornagh	Brampton (gent)	Letton	1681	Receiv./Gen, of Nfk
*Hobart	John	Sir John	Blickling	1682	Lincolns Inn
*Hobart	Thomas	Sir John	Blickling	1682	Lincolns Inn
*Gurdon	John	Brampton(gent)	Letton	1683	
*Long	Thomas	Robert (gent)	Foulden	1684	
Stone	Batholo mew	Batholom.(gent)	Wicklewood	1684	
Seaborne	James	Thomas (gent)	Wymondham	1685	Lincoln's Inn
Long	William	Robert (gent)	Foulden	1685	
Gooch	Thomas	Thomas (attorney)	Hoo, Nfk.	1689	
Gleane	Peter	Thomas (baronet)	Hardwick (Nfk)	1689	Father in Fleet Prison
Wands-worth	Nathan	Nathan (gent)	Intwood	1685	
Talbot	John	Clere (gent)	Wymondham	1687	
Mallom	John	John (gent)	Wacton	1688	
*Clarke	Hezekiah	Richard (clerk Head M)	Wymondham	1688	
Markant	Thomas	Thomas (gent)	Wendling	1690	
Browne	John	Richard (gent)	Scarning	1691	
Stagge	James	John (butcher)	Shipdham		church, HM Saham Sch
Watson	John	John (clerk)	Hingham	1693	Church
King	William	Robert (gent)	Wymondham	1693	
Newman	Thomas	Thomas (gent)	Baconsthorpe	1693	Middle Temple
Rant	William	Humphrey (gent)	Dickleburgh	1694	Church
Watson	John	John (clerk)	Hingham	1695	church in Norfolk
Gillman	Samuel	Samuel(brewer)	Hingham	1695	
*Clarke	Rowland	Richard (clerk HM)	Wymondham	1695	Church
Grigson	Robert	William (clerk)	Morley	1695	

Surname	First name	Father	Home area	Entry Univ	Later position
*brothers					
Jubbs	William	William (gent)	Wymondham	1696	
Goodrich	John	Matthew (surgeon)	Norwich	1698	surgeon?
Stone	Robert	Robert	Wymondham	1700	
Young	Henry	Edmund (innkeeper)	Wymondham	1700	
Knyvett	Thomas	John (weaver)	Fundenhall	1701	
Holmes	Thomas	Thomas (gent)	Mundham Nfk	1701	church in Nfk
Batho	Samuel	Theopholis (draper)	Beccles	1703	
Gibbs	Robert	Stephen (gent)	Wymondham	1703	farmer?
Le Neve	Francis	John, (brewer)	b.Wymondham		
Swift	John	Robert (husbdman)	Kimberley	1706	
Amyas	Benjamin	John (Rct Heth)	Gt. Melton	1707	d.1714
Norris	James	James	Norwich	1708	Church
Blomefield	Thomas	Francis (clothier)	Attleborough	1708	chaplain Duke Dorset
Carver	Philip	Walter (druggist)	Wymondham	1709	church in Nfk
Verdon	John	John (husbandman)	Methwold	1713	church in Nfk
Gleane	Peter	Sir ?	Hardwick	1713	proctor Ct Canterbury
Bourne	John	(tanner)	Wymondham	1713	
Borret	John	John (attorney)	Griston	1714	Church
Fawcett	Horace	Robert (clerk)	Rackheath	1717	church in Nfk.
Hogan	Thomas	Thomas Esq.	Gt. Dunham	1720	died mental disorder
Saltier	Nathaniel	Nathaniel (clerk)	Wymondham	1720	church/master
Day	Barholo mew	John (weaver)	Norwich	1720	MB doctor in Wymond.
Freemoult	Robert	Joel (attorney)	Norwich	1720	Inner temple
Jubbs	Ralph	John (weaver)	Wymondham	1720	
Eglinton	Thomas	Henry (gent)	Bawdeswell	1722	Church
Kirby	Walter	Francis (gent)	King's Lynn	1723	Mayor of Lynn 1744
Wodehouse	William	Sir John (bt)	Kimberley	1723	MP Nfk '34 to 36 d. of small'pox
Knipe	William	Edmund (gent)	Tacolneston	1724	Middle Temple
Negus	Henry	Henry Esq.	Hoveton	1725	Inner Temple
Blanks	John	Christopher (gent)	Bergh Apton	1725	Church
Heighoe	Grigson	Edward (clerk)	Hardingham	1726	Church

Surname	First name	Father	Home area	Entry Univ	Later position
*brothers					
Ducket	Tinkler	Henry (farmer)	Spixworth	1727	priest-expelled
Smith	Peter	James (clerk)	Stow Nfk.	1728	Church
Gibbs	Stephen	Robert(farmer) OB	Wymondham	1729	friend of Ducket
Bond	Thomas	Jonas (grazier)	Lt. Ellingham	1734	Church
Warren	John	John (clerk)	Fornham All Sts	1734	church
Goodwin	Robert	Thomas (surgeon	Lynn	1734	Church
Bullock	Robert	Robert?	Hingham	1738	Lord manor Thuxtons Wym
Carver	Charles	Philip (clerk)	Besthorpe	1741	Church
Story	William	James (A11grazier)	Kimberley	1741	chaplain Wodehouse
Smith	John	John (surgeon)	Wymondham	1751	Church
Heath	William	William (gent)	Hemblington	1753	Church
Candler	Philip	Philip (clerk)	Blofield	1757	Church
Buckle	Stephen	William (grazier)	Crownthorpe	1759	Church
Knopwood	Robert	Robert (gent)	Threxton	1781	Chur. Tasmania
Martin	Wormley	Wormley (clerk)	South Repps	1784	Church
Hepworth	John	Joseph (clerk)	born Wymondham	1788	Church/lect. Greek
Coleby	George	Charles (farmer)	Knapton	1791	Church
Bircham	Charles	William (farmer)	Hackford	1791	d. 1794
Cann	John	John	Wymondham	1808	Church
Jickling	Henry	Nicholas (gent)	b. at Wells	1818	Lincolns Inn
French	William	Samuel (farmer)	Suffolk	1826	Church
Tuck	Thomas	John (gent)	Wilton Nfk	1829	Church

Surname	First name	Father	Home area	Entered school	
Camp	Henry	George (Carpenter)	Wymondham	1870	
Smith	Frederick (10)	John Robert	Wymondham	1870	
Smith	William(9)	(shopkeeper)	Wymondham	1870	
Hare	John	John (farmer)	Wymondham	1870	
Barker	Charles(13)	John	Suton	1871	
Barker	Francis(11)	John	Suton	1871	
Garrett	George	(miller)	Silfield	1871	
Banham	Thomas(10)	Henry (miller & farmer)	Wymondham	1871	
Taylor	Robert(11)	Willm. bank agent	Wymondham	1871	
Colman	William(11)	J. R. (builder) grandfather	Wymondham	1873	

Surname	First name	Father	Home area	Entered school	Later position
Colman	James (10)	J R (builder) grandfather	Wymondham	1873	
Cleveland	Robert (8)		Wymondham	1873	
Jermyn	Henry	Vincent (farmer)	Wymondham	1873	
Cleveland	Arthur		Wymondham	1874	
Wood	Henry	James	Wymondham	1874	
Tudden ham	William	William (butcher)	Wymondham	1876	
Tillet	Arthur	John (Kings Head)	Wymondham	1878	
Knivett	William	(baker)	Wymondham	1878	
Semmence	Albert B.		Wymondham		d in action 1915
Cook	Ernest		Hingham		d at Somme

With a few exceptions, all the above students attended university, going up to Gonville and Caius College, Cambridge, as did most students from East Anglia during the seventeenth and eighteenth centuries.

Graduands of Gonville and Caius College processing in 2005. (Photograph used by kind permission of Professor W. Y. Liang)

It is very difficult to find evidence of Wymondham Grammar School boys in the earlier periods of its history. Those who went up to University had their names officially recorded in the Cambridge and Oxford Year Books, which can be found in University Libraries. Little can be discovered of those who did not.

We are more fortunate with the later periods, particularly the nineteenth century, for which there are many more records available.

Below is a list of pupils in the school in 1892, probably in order of merit.

VI	Wilcox	Skinner
Howlet I	Taylor iii	Clowes
Hanworth I	Palmer ii	
Tomlins	Winearls	**I**
	Groom	Smith viii
V	Fulcher	Glasspoole
Waiwright i	Smith v	Rushmer
McMullon ii		Barker iii
Hughes viii	**II**	Shockley
Hill	Sleigh	Clare
Hanwoth ii	Cremer I	Bagshaw iii
Bagshaw ii	Wainwright ii	Gilbert
Howlett ii	Semmence	Smith ix
Shepherd	Parker	Hanworth iii
	Taylor iv	Hanworth iv
IV	Ling	Cremer ii
Mace	Millard	Barker iv
Clements	Lewis i	
Smith iii	Howard	
Welton	Wright i	
Coleman	Wright ii	

Lot No in 1839	Approx. Size	Nature	Position	Tenant in 1839	Tenant in 1913	Income in 1913
Town Lands						
1	7 Acres	Arable	Near Bolton's Mill, Suton	Esau Bolton	William Harrison	£10 10s
2	12 Acres	Arable	Suton	William Ringer	Elijah Ely	
3	10 Acres	Arable	Suton	Saul Standforth	Elijah Ely	£20 7s
4	18 Acres	Arable	Adjoining The Lizard	Anthony Bunn	Henry Jermyn	£18 11s 4d
5	3 Acres	Arable	In Park Field	Mary Cross	William Coffin	£5 5s
6	3 Acres	Arable	Adjoining Nch Rd	William Jermyn	C R Ayton	£6 10s
7	3 Acres	Arable	Near Bellrope Lane	James Humphreys	T Green	£5 5s
8	2 Acres	Pasture	In Folly Lane	Thomas Mayes	Alice Standley	£8
9	1 Acre	Pasture	Adjoining above	Thomas Mayes	W. J. Browes	£4
10	1 Acre	Arable	In Chapel Lane	Baxter Money	Unlet	
11	1 Acre	Meadow	Near Chapel Bridge	John Bunn	Unlet	
12	30 Acres	Arable	In North Field	Thomas Bayley et al	Richard Standley	£40
13	1 Acre	Arable	At Kidd's Moor	Mr. Wright	W. Thompson	£1 10s
Fuel Lands						
14	16 Acres	Arable	Near Brinn's Lane	Mr. Wight		
15	15 Acres	Arable	Adjoining above	Miller Race		
Buildings etc						
Cottage			At The Lizard		George Stubbs	£5
Allotments					Daynes & Carpenter	£6 14s 8d
Warehouses			Town Green	Cornelius Tipple		
House & garden		Headmaster's House	Town Green		Rev. E. C. Brown	£20
Land+Gymnasium			Town Green		Church Club	£8
Consols	£691 6s 5d				Official Trustees	£17 5s 8d

Wymondham Town Lands and their allocation 1839 and 1913

BIBLIOGRAPHY

MANUSCRIPTS

Wymondham Town Archive

The Town Book 1583-1627, transcribed by J. H. Wilson

Many original documents and letters, formerly in the possession of Mr. Bernard Gledhill

Messrs. Pomeroy & Sons

Wymondham Grammar School Foundation Cash Book, 1889 - 1963

Minute book of Wymondham Old Grammar School Endowment, 1912 - 1944

Terrier, Grammar School and Fuel Allotment Trusts (1893)

ARTICLES

T. Hugh Bryant, 'The Churches of Norfolk', in *Norwich Mercury* Jan 20th, Jan 27th, Feb 3rd, 1906.

M. F. Lloyd Pritchard, 'The Education of the Poor in Norfolk', in *Norfolk Archaeology* Volume 33 (1962-1965)

M. F. Lloyd Pritchard, 'The Misappropriation of Scarning School', in *Notes and Queries* Volume 195 (1950)

UNPUBLISHED WORKS

Mary Garner, 'Wymondham's Town Lands Charity in the Eighteenth Century'.

Percy Millican, 'Becket's Chapel, Wymondham'

H. W. Saunders, 'A History of Norwich Grammar School'.

N. H. Williams, 'The History of Wymondham Grammar School'.

BOOKS

C. Barringer, R. Fowle, S. Spicer (ed), *Wymondham in the Seventeenth Century* (Wymondham 1993)

David Birt, *Elizabeth's England* (Longman, 1981)

Francis Blomefield, *An essay towards a topographical history of Norfolk* (Volume II London 1805)

E. H. Carter, *The Norwich Subscription Books* (Nelson 1937)

Robert Ralston Cawley, *Henry Peacham, His Contribution to English Poetry* (Pennsylvania State University Press 1971)

Rae P. Collins, *A Journey in Ancestry* (Sutton Publishers Gloucs. 1984)

C. Davison & R. Pestell, *Wild Waxham* (2004)

Brenda Garrard, *Wymondham Parish Gilds in the Early Sixteenth Century* (Reeve 2003)

Alan Hughes (ed), *Titus Andronicus* (The New Cambridge Shakespeare 1994)

Helen M. Jewel, *Education in Early Modern England* (Macmillan Press Ltd 1998)

G. P. Jones & A. G. Pool, *A Hundred Years of Economic Development in Great Britain (1840 - 1940)* (Duckworth 1940)

R. W. Ketton-Cremer, *Norfolk in the Civil War* (Faber and Faber 1969)

Henry Peacham *The Complete Gentleman and other works* (The Folger Shakespeare Library, New York 1962)

Henry Peacham, *Minerva Britanna 1612* (The Scholar Press 1969)

Michael Sanderson *Education, Economic Change and Society in England 1780 - 1870 (*Economic History Society 1983)

D. W. Sylvester, *Educational Documents 800-1816* (Methuen 1970)

John Venn, *Biographical History of Gonville and Caius College 1349 - 1897* (2 volumes. CUP 1898)

W. A. L. Vincent, *The Grammar Schools* (John Murray 1969)

F. Watson, *The English Grammar Schools to 1660* (CUP 1908)

Wodehouse John, Earl of Kimberley *The Wodehouses of Kimberley* (Chiswick Press 1887)

Index